GROWING A BUSINESS

GROWING A BUSINESS

Paul Hawken

COLLINS
PUBLISHERS

First published in Canada 1987
by Collins Publishers
100 Lesmill Road, Don Mills, Ontario

Canadian Cataloguing in Publication Data
Hawken, Paul.
  Growing a business

ISBN 0-00-217903-2

1.New business enterprises.   2.Small business—Management.   I.Title.

HD62.5.H39   1987   658.1'1   C87-094476-2

Printed and bound in the United States of America

To Gordon Sherman, who gave his best to business and was the best business had to give

CONTENTS

1

Something
You Live
to Do

WHEN I started my first company in Boston twenty years ago, I had little interest in business. I was just trying to restore my health. Hindered by asthma since I was six weeks old, I had begun experimenting with my diet and discovered a disquieting correlation. When I stopped eating the normal American diet of sugar, fats, alcohol, chemicals, and additives, I felt better. I could breathe freely. When I tried to sneak in a hamburger and a Coke, my body rebelled. After a year of going from one diet to the other, I was left with a most depressing conclusion: if I wanted to be healthy, I'd have to become a food nut. I bid a fond farewell to my junk foods but then discovered that a steady diet of natural food was impossible to obtain without spending ten hours a week shopping at ethnic food stores, farm stands, Seventh-Day Adventist flour mills, Japan Town, and other distant vendors. The health food stores certainly weren't very helpful. For the most part, their idea of food included high-priced nostrums and vitamin formulas—sold by women who wore nurses' uniforms and white hosiery that made their legs look slightly cadaverous.

Tired of spending so much time shopping, I started the first natural foods store in Boston, and one of the first in the country. In the first year of operation on Newbury Street, it grossed about $300 a day and I had fun doing it. The smallness of the operation allowed me to feel close to customers and suppliers. When the business began to grow and I had to spend more time behind a desk than behind a counter, I enjoyed it less. As the years rolled by, the company made money, lost it, hired hundreds of employees, bought railroad cars, opened stores and warehouses on both coasts, set up wholesale and manufacturing facilities, flirted with bankruptcy, and engendered a host of lean and hungry-looking competitors—some of them friends and former associates.

Along the way I managed to commit most of the original sins of commerce. I overborrowed, understaffed, undermanaged, overstaffed, and overstocked. I managed to alienate most of my staff at one time or another, failed to delegate efficiently, and didn't know how to read the balance sheet. (I can read a balance sheet now, but I'm still capable of making these other mistakes.)

When I sold the business after seven years, Erewhon

Trading Co. was grossing $25,000 a day. That was in 1973. I departed the country and took up the pen—something I had always wanted to do—in order to write a book about a community in Scotland. When I returned to the States a couple of years later, with an Australian wife I had met in Scotland, I discovered another reason to go into business for myself: I was unemployable. I had not held a salaried job in my adult life, had no college degree, and my experience in running a company was not deemed sufficient qualification for a position in corporate America. I didn't fill any job description. I checked the want ads in the Sunday papers but didn't find anybody who wanted me to start a business for them. Not wanting to go back to college to get a job description, I went back into business. In the parlance of the day, I became an entrepreneur—again.

But only indirectly: at first I consulted and worked with companies in the food, publishing, and waste conversion fields, and I did three turnarounds for companies in deep trouble, one each in fashion, marketing, and energy. I wrote a book about the effect that individuals, as opposed to institutions, have on the future. After three years of free-lance problem solving, my friend Dave Smith and I founded Smith & Hawken. That was eight years ago, and our office in Mill Valley, California, is where you'll find me today.

This book comes straight from those business experiences. When I started the natural food business in Boston, my business knowledge was scant. I did the best I could and began reading everything I could lay my hands on. I subscribed to *The Wall Street Journal*. It confused me. I read the major business magazines. Their *Fortune* 500 world seemed irrelevant. I sneaked into classes at the Harvard Business School. Their case studies were lunar in their usefulness to my enterprise. The more I searched, the more confused I became. The more exposure I gained to the "official" world of business, the more I began to doubt that I was in business at all. I seemed to be doing something entirely different. I get that same feeling today when I read most of the standard business literature.

I believe that most people in new businesses, and some in not-so-new businesses, have the same problem. They don't feel connected to the conventional wisdom of the books, TV shows, video cassettes, expensive training seminars, and consulting services that compete for our attention. Much of the material is self-evident—be honest, find a gap in the market, the customer comes first, hire well, and so on—and other advice seems to be diluted from the experience of big businesses, as if a small business is just a flake chipped off the larger corporate world.

That leaves you and me out, but we are the people who run most of the businesses in this country, or soon will. According to David Birch, a researcher at MIT, using figures supplied by Dun & Bradstreet, there were two hundred thousand business start-ups in this country in 1965. We are now seeing a start-up rate of nearly seven hundred thousand a year. Subtract inactive companies, add in partnerships and sole proprietorships, and the total number of new businesses started in 1986 was over 1 million, almost half of them by women. The emergence of women in entrepreneurship in America is perhaps the greatest advantage now enjoyed by the American economy, which, alone among the world's economies, encourages this development.

Birch's studies show that these small businesses have been the driving force in economic growth and job creation in the United States since the mid-seventies. From oblivion, if not disgrace, to an almost hackneyed stardom, small business has come into its own in the last twenty-five years. Thirty-seven percent of all employed men and nearly half of the working women want or intend to start a business. The future of American business is standing at the threshold, not sitting in the boardrooms.

This movement toward new enterprise must reflect a certain amount of alienation of the work force from the conditions of their jobs. It is possible for the assembly-line worker consigned to tightening the bolts on the transmission and the office worker who processes medical insurance claims to work with pride and efficiency, but it's not easy to maintain that attitude. We were not created in order to spend half or more of our waking lives in such constricting circumstances, and we know it. Conformity within a large bureaucracy was the meal ticket for most people in the fifties, but I believe that the ability to strike out on one's own will be the most dynamic means of developing a "career" in the late 1980s and 1990s. This path will lead to the greatest job satisfaction and personal development. Knowing how to grow one's own business will be critical. The person who chooses to hide within some bureaucracy may be left behind.

This is a book about growing that business, with all that the term "growing" implies about paying attention to the world around you, learning from others, and changing yourself. It is based first and foremost on the assumption that you have within you the ideas, knowledge, and skills to be a good businessperson in some area. You know more about starting a business than you think you do. And you'll learn faster than you might think you can.

Much of what you will read in this book will not match up with the conventional wisdom (although you should read as many other books as you can; the more you take in, the more you will be able to distinguish convention from common sense). I will rebut some of the jargon and advice running amok today. For example, many experts say that young businesses go under most often because they lack sufficient capital. I believe that, for the new and growing business, *too much money* is a greater problem than too little, and I'll explain why in a later chapter. Some books claim that innovation and the entrepreneurial mind are "techniques" that can be learned from books or in a classroom. I don't think so. The innovative mind is nurtured by experience, not by textbooks.

This is not a how-to manual or a step-by-step guide to starting your own business. There are other books that are guides, and some of them are good. What is missing are books by people who are in small and medium-sized businesses and who intend to stay there—straight talk about what works and what doesn't, and why.

All businesses involve such factors as cash flow, accounting, and marketing. These determine whether the business is allowed to carry out the larger function of meeting needs by providing goods and services. But these things no more describe your business than household shopping lists and errands describe your family. This book will discuss the structure and mechanics of business, to be sure, but always with an eye toward affirming your own common sense and intentions. I want to demystify, not with a set of dictums and executive summaries, but with a book that illustrates how the successful business is an expression of a person.

I do not arbitrarily restrict my focus to small businesses. Stewart Brand, publisher of the *Whole Earth Catalog* and the *Whole Earth Review*, was nosing around the Smith & Hawken offices when he came across the customer service principles I discuss in a later chapter. The principles are the work of our vice president, Lew Richmond. Write these up and publish them, Stewart suggested. The magazine piece based on them and titled "You Are the Customer, You Are the Company" was the most widely reprinted article I have published. The majority of the requests for it came from *Fortune* 500 companies, illustrating the fact that the needs of and differences among large, medium, and small businesses are less distinct than we sometimes suppose. Within the structure of every company or conglomerate are ten, fifty, five hundred, even a thousand units in the big business that function as small businesses, engaged in everything from shipping and manufacturing to planning, hiring, and custodial work. There's no reason why every department in a corporation can't be a well-run small business.

This book is written for that corporate audience, too. Most of us in businesses large or small have the same problems and similar means at our disposal to solve them: energy, ingenuity, and common sense. Big businesses sometimes get bogged down in procedures, policies, and flow charts, but when the problems are solved as opposed to shuffled, I believe they're solved by people using their heads, not handbooks.

We must learn how to grow our businesses—small, large, and small-within-large—more successfully and more humanely. American businesses employ our people, maintain and raise the standard of living, and give us the technical and practical means to solve our problems. For the first time in my forty-year lifetime, people are standing up in large numbers and saying a simple and vitally important thing: *Being a good human being is good business*. And like no other endeavor in our lives, business impels us into the society at large, with prospects of betterment for all concerned. I don't believe that the explosion in entrepreneurial business in the United States is merely an increase in numbers or a measure of greed. This explosion also represents a search for more meaning in our lives.

Twenty years ago I couldn't have written the previous paragraph. That kind of thinking didn't wash. In 1967, business was suspect. "Dow Shall Not Kill" was a popular slogan of the antiwar movement. Corporate recruiters were run off the campuses of Stanford, Michigan State, Wisconsin, and other universities. Businessmen ranked low in polls of public approval. Most of this animosity was directed against the big companies, but small businesses were also implicated. The word "entrepreneur" was associated with opportunism rather than with the subtly different opportunity.

A few weeks after I opened my store in Boston a friend asked pointblank, "How does it feel to be an entrepreneur?" I was humiliated. Entrepreneurs were folks who sold T-shirts during papal visits or bottled water after natural disasters. They took kittens from the animal shelter and sold them as purebreds or they dyed sparrows yellow and passed them off as canaries. I suddenly realized why my father, a photographer, and my mother, a research assistant, had not been jubilant at my decision to open a store, and wouldn't even tell their friends what I was doing. Since we were recently arrived from England on my father's side, the English stigma about business still adhered. My venture confirmed for my parents that their second-born was a failure, and I thereby fulfilled the promise I had shown since early childhood. I thought of them often as I swept the sidewalk outside my store.

They weren't the only people who flinched at my decision to enter business. Former teachers struggled to maintain a calm expression when I told them I was a storekeeper, friends expressed concern about my "direction in life," and old girlfriends didn't return my calls.

All my friends were antibusiness. In the sixties the Vietnam war was viewed as institutional behavior in its purest form. Government and the military-industrial complex were held equally responsible. My store on Newbury Street in Boston, stocked though it was with the staff of life, might as well have been a weapons laboratory. At least that was the feeling I had. My sense of isolation became so acute I almost joined the Rotary Club.

Some of my friends, who had been appalled by my decision to go into business on my own, looked on matters in a different light some years later, when the first oil-related recession struck in 1974–75. The liberal arts dream was tattered. English majors were looking for jobs and

17

some of them realized what I had discovered: no institution in American life is freer to do what it wants to do than a business, and that includes *creating its own jobs*. I found out that there were hardly any rules governing business, and no regulations to speak of—and my store required the handling of food, one of the most highly regulated of businesses. Despite the grumblings of businesspeople about government intervention and regulation, the fact remains that a business is the most unencumbered institution in the United States. The self-owned and -operated business is the freest life in the world.

I don't believe that the values of the sixties are the motive for entrepreneurial endeavor today. A lot of businesses are started in order to make money, big money, and the sooner the better. Some of the attitudes that seem to have settled into place in the era of Ronald Reagan—greed being one of them—are a far cry from my idea of good business thinking.

Although aware of this discordance, I believe that most, if not all, of the successful new businesses are operating with values that go beyond opportunism. In fact, I believe they're successful *because* they have a broader vision. Seeing the world around you clearly is a critical step in developing an idea for a business, carrying out that idea, and then thriving with an ongoing concern. Through choice, predilection, lack of education, impatience, or other causes, the entrepreneur lives, in a way, outside the mainstream. He or she is in the society but is able to step back and gain a perspective on it: entrepreneurship is a way of seeing before it is a way of acting, and it is a way of acting long before it's a way of doing business.

Most successful new businesspeople do not start out in life thinking that this is what they want to do. Their entrepreneurial ideas spring from a deep immersion in some occupation, hobby, or other pursuit. Spurred by something missing in the world, the entrepreneur begins to think about and envision a product or service, or a change in an existing product or service. The entrepreneur is often the first one to spot the opening, and if things work out that person will have a successful business.

When I started the natural food business, I believed that if I could see the wisdom of changing my eating habits, there were sufficient numbers of other people who would also figure out the advantages of natural food. My business would grow in response to that awareness and be ready to serve those needs.

People intuitively understand that a good business enhances the lives of all who work within it, and enriches the lives of all those who are touched by it. I opened my store in Boston because I needed good food—pure and simple. That operation was a vital part of me. Likewise, the business you can succeed with is distinctly and utterly you and yours. It is unlike any other business in the world. Being in business is not about making money. It is a way to become who you are.

2

Be Careful,
You May Succeed

To SEE the reward of commerce as money and the risk of commerce as failure is to see nothing at all. The bottom line is down where it belongs—at the bottom. Way above it in importance are the infinite number of events that produce the profit or the loss. Business is stunning in its richness and variation. It is a palette far broader than most people seem to believe. But rarely do we hear about what really happens inside business. The whopping success stories are glorified, the failures are dissected or shunned. The rest is silence. Our demand for heroes and goats obscures the truth.

Your business will probably not be a triumph that lands

you on the business page, or an embarrassing failure that leaves a gap in your résumé—unexplained down time—when you slink back to the nine-to-five. Most businesses are just businesses, and not the stuff of *People* magazine. Whatever happens, your first business will be a learning experience like you never expected. I have seen some businesses inch along year after year with great struggle, and others glide into embarrassing prosperity as if such success were the true nature of all things. I have seen some owners bloom and prosper in their enterprises, and others become almost Dickensian in the hardened cynicism they confess was purchased at the counters of commerce.

I offer the following general thoughts in order to help you become better prepared for the rewards and challenges of running your own small business. I hope I don't put you off. My intention is to get you excited.

BEGIN AT THE BEGINNING

Obviously, you say, begin at the beginning, but it's not that easy. I hear business ideas all the time and many of them are good, but the shortcoming I observe most often is that people don't know where to begin. Nor is it simple to give instruction in this regard because every business is so different. One way to approach the problem is by stating what is *not* the beginning. A business plan is not the beginning, nor is money in the bank, a rented space, or the merchandise inside. The beginning is certainly not plush offices, an expensive car for the boss, long lunches out, or any of the other perks that can separate the employees from their boss. (It's bad enough to end up with this separation. It's fatal to start out this way. Many of the trappings people associate with success in business are the vestiges of mature businesses in which the founder is often bored, running on empty, or just superfluous.) The beginning is not a grand, sweeping event. It's certainly not a Grand Opening. That's closer to the end than the beginning.

To find the beginning, reduce your business idea to its apparent essence. Then reduce it again. A nationwide chain must begin with the process of establishing a nearly microscopic kernel of what will become that national chain. The beginning anticipates, in an almost genetic fashion, the business it will become. Each step in the growth of a business is a consequence of the preceding step. I have always believed that when the proper order is correctly identified, a business is almost failure-proof. Don't cut a single corner along the way. Cutting that first corner is a beginning of a different sort—the beginning of failure.

To start and grow a business, you have to get down and dirty. I don't mean merely hands-on, but with your whole body, mind, and soul. If a business is to grow you have to own it—the acts, habits, functions, jobs, and grunt labor. By beginning at the beginning, you will be able to control it with a finer hand. You have to know all the fundamental details in order to give them away later. Any attempt to bypass the seminal processes will result in trouble later on because the beginning determines all that follows. Most successful businesses started from extremely humble origins. John Deere was a blacksmith from Vermont who designed a better plow after moving to Illinois. The company he founded celebrated its one hundred fiftieth year in 1987. In 1925, C. E. Wollman was an agricultural engineer experimenting with aerial crop dusting in Louisiana. It wasn't until 1966 that Delta Air Lines went out of the crop-dusting business. Dart-Kraft started as a horse and wagon. Kellogg's started as an offshoot of a sanitarium by selling wheat flakes. Coca-Cola was a rather quackish cure-all sold over the counter in an Atlanta pharmacy. Levi Strauss started when a German immigrant was overstocked with tent canvas during the California Gold Rush and turned the material into miners' pants.

ENTREPRENEURS ARE RISK-AVOIDERS

The common wisdom holds that entrepreneurs love to take risks. That's mostly hype. Their acts may appear risky in comparison with corporations, which are so large they should be willing to take risks, rather than trying to insure they lose nothing. The entrepreneur has the freedom of anonymity in which to accomplish something.

Once the entrepreneur has seen how to create a product or service to meet demand—whether it is the home computer (Apple Computer) or a hub-and-spoke air delivery system (Federal Express), or housewives' needs for aerobic exercise (Jane Fonda)—much of what the outsider perceives as risk in the situation is erased. Alice Medrich, co-founder of Cocolat, the multimillion-dollar California dessert bakery, opened her first store in Berkeley without any concern for the risk involved. She knew her chocolates were the best and she knew her customers would agree with her. In a way, she acknowledges, her confidence might have seemed arrogant to an observer.

Alice Medrich saw opportunity, not risk. She exemplifies the idea put forward by Lyle Spencer of McBer and Company, a business consulting firm: "The entrepreneur will take what seems from the outside to be a wild risk. But his high self-confidence means that it does not seem such a great risk to him. Because he believes in himself so much, he calculates the odds differently."

If you persist in seeing a situation in terms of risk, look again. If you still see risk instead of opportunity, walk away, because you just might be right.

BUSINESS IS FRIGHTENING

No matter how well he or she has pursued a course of risk-avoidance, the entrepreneur must expect at some time to experience an awful emptiness in the pit of the stomach. My first encounter with the loan officer at the New England Merchant's Bank in Boston was essentially humiliating. He was a sandy-haired Brahmin with the imposing name of John Crocker Bigelow. Clearly, a vice president on the way up.

Fortunately, he and his wife were also customers of the Erewhon store. Nevertheless, as I sat before his desk I was nervous as a bridegroom, for the simple reason that I had no idea what to do or say. I needed a loan. If I didn't get the money, I was out of business. John asked me about the wholesale business and I prattled on about protein content of hard red wheats from Montana, the difference between impeller-pressed and solvent-extracted oils, the use of biodynamic inoculants in our composted steer manure, and other details sure to impress him with my grasp of the business.

John smiled. He asked me what my cash flow looked like for next year, what my "quick ratio" was, and how I was doing on the aging of receivables. I didn't know what any of those terms meant. In fact, I hadn't even heard of them. I turned the color of my red wheat and to this day have no idea what I said. To John's credit and my everlasting relief, he gave Erewhon the loan anyway. But I'll never forget the embarrassment.

Even if your family, friends, and associates and employees (if any) are all-out supportive, even if nothing goes wrong at first (unimaginable), you will feel a strange loneliness. A time will come when the primal fears emerge: What have I done? Isn't someone else doing it, too, and better?

You will almost certainly develop the "looking-over-your-shoulder" syndrome. For the first two years of Smith & Hawken's existence I was convinced that one day someone would innocently ask, "Have you seen Kelly's tool catalog? It's a lot like yours. They're in Pennsylvania." And I would open that catalog and there I would be—in second place. If the Erewhon natural foods store in Boston had one advantage, it was that I was so familiar with the turf I knew I had found virgin territory. But of course that assurance just left me open to the inevitable fear, "Why is it wide open out there? Why hasn't anyone done it before?"

In the instance of a more prosaic venture, such as a bookstore, a pizza parlor, or a hairdresser, the doubts will be, "Why isn't anyone doing it this way already—or in this location—or with this recipe, which is so obviously superior?"

Farming may be the diciest of any small business, requiring more talent and skills than one person can reasonably expect to possess, as well as an acute sensitivity to the immediate environment. The farmer is proverbially at the mercy of market and natural forces utterly beyond his control. I have felt that way about all my businesses, and you will probably feel the same way about your enterprise. So, the final fear to which all new businesspeople are prey comes from realizing that, although you are doing the best you can and working as well as you know how, you are always about *this far* from possible failure.

Fear of failure may or may not be helpful, but it is rational. Every businessperson, no matter how intelligent and resourceful, can and will fall prey to delusion and misjudgment. If you are moving from the structured comfort of an established institution to a small business of your own, you have lost the buffer the institution provides between a mistake and total failure.

None of these fears is easy to talk about. When you try, you may receive some lame, halfhearted advice. Your family and friends certainly aren't trying to hurt you. They just don't have the same frame of reference. They may think that, well, you're out there trying to make money, it was your decision to do it, it's not as though your boss is coming down on you. It's your problem. After a while, you may quit talking to friends about your business. At least your fears will have the dignity of silence.

You may believe my scenario is an exaggeration because I started out when entrepreneurship wasn't accepted. But although entrepreneurship is accepted now, it's still not understood.

BUSINESS TESTS CHARACTER

Business tests character like no other endeavor I know, and it reveals it, too.

The moment you enter the world of business—as a provider, not merely as a consumer—you will have a hundred opportunities a day to act beneficially or wrongly, to deal with people fairly or otherwise, to enhance your social environment or pollute it. Imagine your favorite store in which the people are kind and responsive. Imagine the opposite store. Now imagine your own store or warehouse or factory. Every business presents the same choices.

The following story is true. Only the nature of the business has been changed.

A plumber who has been scratching out a decent living for ten years comes up with the good, though not original, idea of selling maintenance contracts that provide free plumbing repairs for one year for seven hundred households who pay a $100 annual fee. Parts are an additional charge, but are discounted. The idea catches on, the business expands, the plumber buys more trucks. A business journalist writes a story about NO-KLOG with its cute motto "No more money down the drain." Calls pour in from plumbers around the country wanting to create a similar business, so the owner starts a franchising operation.

Within five years, he has eight hundred authorized franchises around the country. He is paying himself a salary in the medium to high six figures. His stock in the company is worth millions, and he has a new twelve-bedroom home, a country house, a small plane, a fleet of cars, and a tidy supply of his newfound love, hand-rolled Monte Cristo cigars.

But things begin to change. Employees who used to like him become fearful and resentful. His franchisees, appreciative at first, now think he's a jerk. His suppliers have gone sour on him because he nickel-and-dimes them to death on every invoice. His wife has left him, his kids are spoiled, he's overweight, and he takes medication for high blood pressure and sedatives to help him sleep. A former stockholder is suing him because he feels he was cheated early on.

Enterprise Week, the pseudonymous national magazine for the "entrepreneurial spirit," features this magnate as one of the year's outstanding success stories. He is proud of the piece and orders a thousand reprints to send to employees, suppliers, and various news services and trade journals.

Like the plumber, your character will be tested by your business. Furthermore, you will have to deal with customers, suppliers, and businesspeople under similar pressure. Some of them won't have your best interests at heart—or those of the society at large. We all know what money can do to people, but as a businessperson you will encounter some of the strangest behavior you've ever seen. You will be incredulous to see people you thought you knew and trusted—good people, really—

become remarkable manipulators of truth and reality. Business is people. Expect the unexpected.

A certain degree of cynicism will come in handy. Cynicism has an undeserved, bad reputation because it often takes the form of untrammeled self-permissiveness in government or the stock market, where it may be an evil. In a subtler form, however, cynicism can add tensile strength to your idealism and your sense of good. With a smattering of cynicism, you will not be swept aside by displays of human venality, and you will be enriched by seeing the world the way it is.

Try to maintain your sense of humor. After Ben Cohen and Jerry Greenfield were firmly established with their Vermont-based Ben & Jerry's Homemade ice cream, a competitor with an ice cream in similar packaging—a knockoff, frankly—journeyed to Vermont and told Ben and Jerry that the two companies should merge. "Wouldn't you rather work with me than against me?"—that oft-uttered threat in the world of commerce. Ben rubbed his beard and told his competitor, "You know, my girlfriend and I have been living together for six years, and we're still not married. I only met you twenty minutes ago."

BUSINESS IS PLAY

The discussion begins, once again, with failure. The most basic way a business can fail is pretty obvious: no customers—the market is unmoved by your overtures. You're not selling anything. Although your widget is good and useful and you are satisfied with the basic setup of your business, there's a missing piece of the puzzle.

My recommendation is simple: *play with it.*

You have gone into business to discover, change, serve, inform, transform, improve, and delight someone. You won't sell to this person otherwise. Examine that list of words and you'll realize that they are all encompassed by one other word: *play.*

The play of a child is full of awe, surprise, doubt, and curiosity. It teaches and inspires. A good school makes learning into a game, engaging everyone, excluding no one, honoring all, ridiculing none. Business is the entrepreneur's playground. Children pepper us with the question "Why?" The entrepreneur asks "Why not?"

Be the customer. Go outside and look back through the window of your small business. Be a child trying to figure out how the world works. Go to a crowded park on a sunny day. Don't go into the back room to read another book about business (even this one).

John P. Stack, president of the Springfield Remanufacturing Center Corp. in Missouri, has turned that entire operation into The Great Game of Business. Stack headed a small group of employees who purchased SRC from International Harvester, its parent company, in 1983. As a subsidiary of IH, the remanufacturing operation had been losing money, but Stack was convinced the numbers could be turned around by involving everyone at the plant in the effort, and the simplest way to do this, Stack believed, was to make a game out of it, and make the game fun to play. Today, almost every conceivable activity of the manufacturing process is quantified—from labor utilization rates to the waste factor on work gloves—and the employees play the game by improving on their scores. Stack quips that walking through one of the three SRC plants is like being in the middle of a bingo game.

Bonuses, promotions, and contributions to the employee stock ownership plan are the tangible results of a good inning or quarter, but the deeper meaning of the SRC way of rebuilding diesel engines is the satisfaction the employees get from meaningful involvement in the functions and success of their business (there is minimal job turnover). No one at SRC is standing out in right field for the whole game, much less sitting in the dugout, contributing nothing. Everybody gets to play.

BUSINESS IS PRACTICE

When you start your business, you may not be as well informed as others. You will have to do things over and over until you get them right, but this will not be rote work. You will have to change as you go. But imagine the opposite. You know everything. You have no opportunity to learn and change. What would be the point?

Business is not about theories or the testing of revolutionary ideas. It is about practice. Ideas and intelligence and creativity, yes, but with a lot of sheer practice thrown in. For years Alice Medrich of Cocolat had difficulty scheduling all of the supplies and staffing needs for the firm's three big holidays of the year—Christmas, Easter, and Valentine's Day. In the beginning, the holidays were a disaster. After a couple of years of practice things ran a little more smoothly in the bakery. Perhaps half a dozen years were required to reach a level of performance Medrich was happy with (remember, only three opportunities a year).

Business is no different from learning to play the piano or to ride a surfboard. With most activities there is no presumption of excellence in the beginning—just the opposite—but many newcomers suppose that they should sit down at the desk on the first day and become Super-businessperson, in full command of the situation.

Relax. Take your time. Work and practice and learn.

TOO MUCH MONEY IS WORSE THAN TOO LITTLE

Money gets a whole chapter later on, but I would like to make you feel better about it right now. It's true: for the small business, too much money is worse than too little. I disagree with the old saw that the major problem afflicting small businesses is a lack of capital. The major problem affecting businesses, large or small, is a lack of *imagination,* not capital. A ready supply of too much money in start-ups tends to replace creativity. Companies with money buy solutions by buying consultants, lawyers, clever accountants, publicity agents, marketing studies, and on and on. Companies without money dream and imagine. Hunger speeds things right along.

Ben & Jerry's started their ice cream business on a shoestring, and so they were unable to purchase an image in the marketplace. Having no choice but to be what they were—Ben and Jerry selling ice cream—their message was unpretentious and "down home," to use Ben's term. Looking back, they can now see that not being able to create an image was probably their greatest asset because its homeyness implied quality and trust.

When Smith & Hawken began, we might have had a little more money than Ben & Jerry's, but not enough to spend on designers, photographers, copywriters, or consultants for our catalog. We did it ourselves or not at all. Because we started out that way, we haven't changed, and we learn new things we'd miss if we jobbed it out.

I never thought much about this in-house advantage until 1985, when a friend launched a new catalog company. He started with an initial mailing of 500,000 catalogs (our first effort had been 487), which he hired a large company in Dallas to create. My friend and I were having lunch when the subject of production costs came up. I asked him how much he spent and he replied nearly $100,000 for production alone. He noticed me choking on my *dim sum* and he asked how much my last catalog had cost (by this time Smith & Hawken was up to about 1 million circulation). I suggested we break the costs down.

His photography cost $25,000. Ours cost $4,000.

His copywriting cost $12,000. I did all of ours.

His layout and design team ran $25,000. Our in-house labor came to $6,000.

He paid $15,000 for typography. We paid $2,700.

He paid $5,000 for a stylist. I asked who or what that is.

He paid $82,000 in total. Our catalog cost us $12,700 for the same number of products and pages.

It's not coincidental that my friend's company is not in business today. He got further faster in the beginning because he had more money to spend, but he thereby forfeited a critical amount of self-education and development.

Politicians like to come up with plans to extend credit to small businesses. This is fine because we need some money, but I'm afraid these good intentions plant a dangerous notion that money solves problems. More money for small businesses will not create jobs or foster innovation. It might even impede these developments. If money could solve problems, there would be no small businesses because the big businesses with plenty of money would run everything.

Small businesses, at least entrepreneurial ones, are formed in order to address problems that money alone *cannot* solve.

NO ONE IS IN CHARGE

As you get involved in business and slowly rise into the stellar world of commerce and finance and deal with bankers and the like, you will notice that, as in Gertrude Stein's epigram about Oakland, there is no *there* there. No commercial mecca, no sages a lot smarter than you, no litany or secrets. Even if you should reach the very top of financial and corporate America, you'll find people like you find on the local school board. It's just us. People will try to throw jargon at you, drown you in their superior knowledge, impress you with their worldwide contacts. Their limos will be long, offices high, expense accounts generous. But underneath that veneer, the judgment and intelligence of the best and the brightest that *Forbes* has to offer are about on a par with what you find in daily life. These people are still practicing, too. Never be intimidated.

The world of commerce is so complex and is changing so quickly that no one in a large corporation is on top of the situation. Many of the captains of industry are just hanging on for the ride. Not long ago, a vice president of chemical giant Union Carbide confessed that the executives of the company had "no idea how to manage a large corporation." And he said this before the catastrophe in Bhopal. Even a clear-cut problem is often beyond management's power to solve, given the complexities of the corporate systems.

The logistics of a large corporation are staggering. The variables involved in running it are beyond the computing power of the biggest computer—forgetting even the minor fact that many of those variables are human. Running even a relatively smaller *Fortune* 500 company such as Apple Computer is so complex it makes the conquests of Alexander the Great seem like child's play. The stories in the newspapers and magazines about the omniscient genius at X,Y,Z Corp. are good copy and little more, intended to appeal to the reader's own dreams of glory. Don't be fooled.

In contrast, the owner of a small business can luxuriate in the relative control he or she has over the operation. But as the business grows, the entrepreneur will slowly become aware of the appropriateness of the root word of "corporation," *corpus,* which means body. If the business gets large enough, it takes on a life of its own and the founder becomes a passenger on the host.

BUSINESS WILL ALWAYS
HAVE PROBLEMS

On an autumn Saturday several years ago, I was working in my office while the rest of the world was enjoying the Indian summer. I forget the particular problem I was trying to solve. It was one of hundreds and I was proceeding in my usual fashion: solve that problem once and for all. For years I had been the greyhound chasing the rabbit of permanent solutions. I knew that if I worked just a little harder, a little longer, a little more creatively, I would finally catch that rabbit and have a perfectly running business at last. I would experience commercial nirvana, and emerge from the dark night of the ledgerbook into the clear dawn of administrative beatitude. Monday morning would always be a pleasure. I was wrong.

I had my nirvana, all right, but it was the opposite of what I had been seeking. On that pretty afternoon the actual truth finally struck me: I would always have problems. In fact, problems signify that the business is in a rapid learning phase. The revelation was liberating. I couldn't understand why other people hadn't told me this earlier. Surely someone had noticed the stupidity of my previous approach to problems. They must have whispered to friends, "What a shame Paul doesn't know."

On Monday morning I looked around at my employees. They knew. I was the last to be clued in. Don't make the same mistake. Understand in the beginning that you will always have problems. It is there that the opportunities lie. A problem is an opportunity in drag.

A mess is a pile of opportunities in drag. Stay in the

mess. Love that mess. It's the only way to straighten it out. This can be a hard lesson to learn because most of us avoid single problems, much less big messes of them. We prefer our lives to be tidy and predictable. Businesspeople feel exactly the same way. We are taught that orderliness is the way to success: hospital corners and accurate books. This is commendable for housekeeping and bookkeeping, but it has to be watched on a conceptual level. A new business simply will not conform to any set of expectations, predictions, or patterns. It will have frayed edges, surprises, and unintended consequences. This is a reflection of the world, and not necessarily some malfunction in your business.

There is a well-known Jungian analyst who, in recounting his experiences with an array of patients, noted that most came to him with a laundry list of problems: their mates were not their friends, their jobs were uninteresting, life in the city was difficult, their health was bad, times were tough. In the early years of his practice, the analyst at first believed that his job was to help these men and women "adjust" to the world. Years later, he realized that his patients were right. Their world wasn't so great. Marriages were almost necessarily precarious, many children were delinquent, schools were like prisons, politicians were corrupt, the air was filthy, and people on the streets were often mean. In short, life was difficult.

In light of his "discovery," the analyst switched his way of dealing with the patients. He no longer worked to help them "adjust." He encouraged them to recognize that their sensitivity to the world was normal. He believed that as they became more, not less, sensitized to their environment, they would start to do something about the problems rather than act the victim all the time. The answer for them was to challenge the world, not to adjust to it passively.

When your business encounters problems and messes, stay with them. Find something valuable down in the dreck. Work with it until you know that mess so well it will never develop again, until it has become your friend. One of the greatest errors of much business literature today is its attempt to instill certainty with checklists, must-dos, the "motherhoods," ten principles, axioms galore, and other assorted truisms. The only axioms I'll throw at you are designed to engage your thinking, not provide easy answers. Business cannot be pinned down this way, and it is rewarding for that very reason.

A few days after my revelation about the nature of problems, an even more important point became clear to me. If I will always have problems, if every business will always have problems, what's the difference between a good business and a bad one?

A good business has interesting problems, a bad business has boring ones. Good management is the art of making the problems so interesting and their solutions so constructive that everyone wants to get to work and deal with them. These problems are like a box of Cracker Jack, containing an extra little charm inside. Bad management involves presenting problems in such a way that people seek to avoid them, put them into memo form, delegate, or toss them into the circular file underneath the desk. Good problems energize. Bad problems enervate.

Some good problems are too much demand for a good product (or not enough demand for a good product), too many opportunities to expand, too many requests for donations, customers showing up on Sunday afternoon seeking a tour of the facility, other people taking credit for your success, having a staff smarter than you are (not at all uncommon), and having a competitor as good as you are, or even better.

Bad problems are too much demand for a product you know is bad, not enough demand for that bad product, hostile customers, outstanding bank loans, and an over-worked, underpaid, unappreciated, and, therefore, dull staff.

Your job as owner and manager is not to solve every problem. Your job is to create a company with compelling problems that attract bright, unusual people to join in solving them. If the problems are too overwhelming, they are corrosive, but if a company is so dull that problems are negligible, your good people will flee, leaving the bureau-crats to run the show.

When you realize that you will always have problems and that it's within your power to make certain they're good ones, you'll never bring them home. You will leave them where they're loved—at work.

Problem solved.

3

Small, Fat, and Happy

A MAJOR COMMERCIAL revolution is taking place in this country. It is vast and pervasive yet we hardly notice it. Large companies have peaked in size and impact. Economic advantage in the marketplace has shifted to small and medium-sized companies. It is important for you, if you have started or are thinking about starting a new business, to understand the opportunity presented by this moment in our economic history. This perspective will help you develop your business idea, and then help you grow that business.

To be specific, here are three important economic changes:

41

1. Products and services must contain more quality and information. We demand it and, in many fields, smaller businesses are in a position to deliver these better goods.
2. The market is becoming so differentiated that size is no longer an advantage. It can be a liability.
3. Passive consumers are being replaced by demanding customers. Big businesses prefer dealing with passive consumers.

THE INFORMATIVE ECONOMY

In *The Next Economy*, I wrote that big business had "peaked" in the United States and was in fact beginning to break up into smaller components. That was in 1983. Before long the Wall Street megamergers and acquisitions began to dominate the news. But I don't believe I was wrong in my prediction. Those Wall Street deals are the symptoms of an old way of doing business. It is precisely because *Fortune* 500 firms cannot find ways to grow that they are beginning to eat their young. For example, from 1978 to 1986, General Motors grew in sales from $63 billion to $102 billion, but the company's share of the domestic car market fell from 48 percent to 39 percent. Price increases, inflation, and acquisitions were the source of GM's "growth."

The net result of the zealous trading, wheeling, and dealing that is front-page news is that the *Fortune* 500 firms have lost between 4 and 6 million permanent jobs since 1970. One million jobs were lost in 1980 alone, when small businesses *added* 2 million jobs. In real terms, adjusted for inflation, the *Fortune* 500 are smaller as an aggregate portion of the U.S. economy than they were twenty years ago.

The economy and the marketplace we are leaving are vestiges of industrialization. Industrialization was essentially the mechanization of traditional methods of work fueled by fossil energy rather than by human energy. You could say that the industrial age was the extension and externalization of our muscles into equipment, machinery, and technology. With the help of machines and technology, the worker accomplished much more than had ever been possible before. It made us prosperous in a way that had never been imagined. Products of higher quality and lower price—better value—were available to more and more people—at first.

Industrialism required a bigger economy with bigger units within it—bigger businesses. Success and scale were practically synonymous. "Big" was good for business and good for the economy. Mass production not only favored scale, it required it. Over five hundred manufacturers jostled for their share of the market in the early days of the car industry in Detroit. Now only three remain.

But the child with his thousand needs and desires matures into the adult. As a postindustrial economy, we are the economic analogue of that adult. The industrial economy matured. We have roads, bridges, airports, and utility grids. We have cars, TVs, and automatic garage door openers. Not everyone has everything he or she needs or wants, but comparatively speaking, and setting aside the question of uneven distribution, North America has most of what it requires on the infrastructural, material level. We don't need the same exponential increases in steel, coal, oil, and electrical production. We don't need another transcontinental highway system. We don't need 140 million more televisions.

I'm not saying that the country doesn't need to grow. We do, but in a different way. We don't need to get bigger in size nor should our desire be simply for more and more. Size and scale have been taken care of. The old industrialism is a victim of its success.

Our economy will not grow bigger in scale, but we will see it become more specific, more diverse, more adapted to individual needs and desires. The economy that served us well is giving way to what I call the *informative* economy.

According to my dictionary, "to inform" means to "imbue or inspire with some specific quality or value." Practically speaking, information is not merely data, telecommunications, or a computer network. It can be these, but it is also the knowledge added to resources to make them valuable. It is design, craft, utility, and durability—everything that makes a product more useful, longer lasting, easier to repair, lighter, stronger, and less energy-consuming. Information is nothing more (or less) than how to make or accomplish something in the best way.

A Chevrolet requires ten to twelve times more expense on warranty repairs than an American-built Honda does. The difference is information in the form of design, workmanship, and quality. Twenty-five years ago Honda was a "small" business. It became a big business not by building bigger cars, or cars with more gadgets, but by building a car with more information. Every small business has that potential advantage because big business, government, labor unions, schools, often don't deliver the goods.

When it comes to housewares, Crate & Barrel of Chicago runs rings around competing department stores and chains. Crate & Barrel is not the biggest housewares store but it is widely acknowledged as the best, with the highest sales per square foot in the industry. The information at Crate & Barrel is the skillful buying developed over twenty-five years of travel and contacts; the best visual displays in the business; a training program second to none; the nicest clerks in town; and superior merchandising, including such touches as the list, posted above the sales counter, of incoming vessels carrying Crate & Barrel goods, port of call, and scheduled date of arrival.

Celestial Seasonings revived the atrophying tea business with "soothing" teas, imaginative recipes, provocative graphics, and direct appeals to the customer's higher sentiments through poems, sayings, and philosophical expressions printed on the tea boxes. The information of Celestial Seasonings is the concern expressed for the health of the tea drinker, the product differentiation to match customers' desires, and package advertising that tries to pry open the heart, not the pocketbook.

When Debbi and Randy Fields started Mrs. Fields Chocolate Chippery they were competing against packaged cookies that were stale, hard, and tasteless. Their recipe was butter, grade A chocolate, sugar, and "just enough flour to hold it together." Mrs. Fields worked in the first cookie store, baked and sold the cookies herself, and stood out on the sidewalk to give away free samples. The information in Mrs. Fields cookies is quality ingredients and generosity with the chocolate, freshness, and paying attention to the customer.

In technology, the informative economy is taking shape through the use of microprocessors, computers, genetic engineering, and robotics. This sector of the economy dominates the headlines about our changing economy, but high tech comprises only 6 percent of the gross national product. The rest of the economy is just as needful of, and just as responsive to, "information-intensive" innovation and entrepreneurship. Whether you are in the outdoor clothing and equipment business like Patagonia, clothing like Esprit de Corp., or diesel engines like the Springfield Remanufacturing Center of Missouri, the market is wide open to products with a higher degree of information.

SIZE IS NO LONGER AN ADVANTAGE

The well-ordered and centralized manufacturing processes of industrial society required bigness and this bigness in turn required uniformity—the mass market. Someone has written that industrialism began the first time a weaver realized he didn't need sheep; he could buy his yarn and free himself from the shackles of the land while concentrating on the vagaries of production.

Modern industrialism began when someone realized that a whole society could want the same product—or at least be induced to buy it. Thus the modern corporation is the result of standardized methods of production. Its strictures, mores, bureaucracies, and marketing schemes derive from the need to produce great numbers of identical products. The degradation of consumer service resulted from the assumption that the customer had to conform to the company, rather than the other way around.

The movement today away from mass markets and mass production means that it is more difficult for a business to please everyone. One size does not fit all, if it ever did. Manifest differences are required in products and services. Gregory Bateson once defined the most elementary unit of information as the "difference that makes a difference." If we are in an economy that is organized increasingly around the amount of information that is in products, rather than around the amount of stuff, then the ability to create differences in manufacturing and delivery of goods and services will be the key to success. This favors smaller businesses or, at the least, businesses with agility, sensitivity, and the ability to listen and respond quickly to the marketplace.

The entrepreneur can more easily produce products with a higher ratio of information—quality—because she is more nimble. Small businesses can think faster, change more quickly, establish better internal communication, and tailor their products and services to smaller markets. We all have to make money in our businesses, but first we have to make a product or deliver a service that people want. Imagination and creativity are more useful than aggressiveness.

Big business has been lagging in the transition from the mass to the informative economy because it cannot *buy* what is needed to make the transition. Products and services of the mass, industrial economy can be broken down into components and quantified in dollars and man-hours. This suited our corporate temperament. But the goal of making a company more intelligent, of bringing together a work force dedicated to the design and production of better products, of maintaining an environment that fosters employee participation and ideas—these elements of business cannot be purchased like new plants, machines, or licenses.

A friend who works at a large think tank was hired a few years ago to fly east and consult with a large baked goods company that wanted to know whether the trend toward lighter, healthier foods with less salt, fat, and sugar was for real or was merely a fad. It's true, his report concluded months later, people really do want to feel better and live longer. The company is still working on a plan to capitalize on its new knowledge. They can afford this time and money because they have lots of products and a famous brand name that are cash cows.

Entrepreneurs don't have to wait for consulting studies. Their stomachs know the answer. They are free to act. Small businesses fly under the commercial radar of the big corporations, free to create their market niche. A Procter & Gamble cannot feasibly downscale in order to address a "mere" $10 million market. The company I work with, Smith & Hawken, will gross around $30 million this year, but we aren't yet large enough in any one product category to give a large company a thought or bother.

Some hopeful businesspeople are stymied because they assume the big companies must know what is going on and must have the answers. In fact, the opposite is the case. Remember that big companies are only that—big.

They are not more efficient, productive, or innovative. In study after study, large businesses score a poor second to small ones in these categories. T. K. Quinn, former chairman of General Electric Credit, once said, "Not a single distinctively new electric home appliance has ever been created by one of the giant concerns—not the first washing machine, electric range, dryer, iron or ironer, electric lamp, refrigerator, radio, toaster, fan, heating pad, razor, lawn mower, freezer, air conditioner, vacuum cleaner, dishwasher, or grill."

Back when Erewhon was a rapidly growing company, I walked into the original store in Boston one day and found four executives of a supermarket chain measuring the store's square footage while tallying register totals on a notepad. They were trying to figure out our sales per square foot, which were phenomenally high for the food industry. Hi, guys. One large cereal company used one of our subsidiary names for an advertising slogan in an effort to reposition its corn flakes in the market. Another cereal company walked off with our logotype and package design without so much as a tip of the hat.

Slow-footedness is embedded in institutional life. The new theories favoring corporate "intrapreneurship" as a means of restructuring and revitalizing commercial institutions ignore a basic dynamic. Entrepreneurial change depends on static situations, and these are provided in abundance by government, large corporations, and other institutions, including educational ones. We need both entrepreneurial and institutional behavior. Each feeds on the other. The role of the former is to foment change. The role of the latter is to test that change.

A case study in this regard is Xerox PARC (Palo Alto Research Corporation), the Silicon Valley research facility designed and funded by Xerox. Its job was to discern the architecture of information in the future, and be the first to invent the office of that future. Located near Stanford University, Xerox PARC attracted many of the brightest minds in the fledgling field of information technology. It worked. By 1974 it had invented the first personal computer, the Alto. Beyond that, Larry Tesler and his associates had also created a computer with a graphic screen, fonts, icons, overlapping windows, pop-up windows, a paint program, and a mouse. You might recognize from that description the Apple Computer's popular Macintosh. But it wasn't the Macintosh. Though it might have been.

When Steve Jobs of Apple toured Xerox PARC in 1979, he saw that Alto computer complete with the mouse. According to Larry Tesler, Jobs was "leaping and jumping around the room and yelling things. He kept saying over and over, 'Why aren't you doing something with this?' The implication was, 'If you don't, we will.' "

Despite the pleading of the staff at Xerox PARC to produce a personal computer for the general market, corporate Xerox in Rochester, New York, saw it as an unacceptable risk. For those executives, the small machine was not a solution to the problem they were working on—offices—and they couldn't see the rest of the world clearly enough. For Steve Jobs, the Macintosh-like computer was the solution to a problem: how to make computers so much fun and easy to use that everyone from kindergartners to professional writers would want to have one.

Jobs was thinking about people. Xerox was thinking about institutions. Had Xerox done any market research, I'm sure it would have verified its decision to forgo development of the computer. At the time, there was no mass market for computers. But how could there have been? People barely knew what computers were. Computers were associated primarily with the space program and airline reservations. But Steve Jobs saw the future more clearly. By envisioning it he helped to create it.

Imagine an ecosystem instead of an economy. Where two ecosystems meet, say the forest and the plains, is a small strip of terrain that conforms strictly to neither system, either in plant or animal life. This margin, an ecotone, as it is called, contains marginal or "edge" species that cannot survive on either side, species of questionable "value." They don't feed the grazing ruminants nor decay into humus on the forest floor. They live, as it were, at the grace of the two larger ecosystems.

But should one of the ecosystems change suddenly, devastated by disease, perhaps, or by some rapid change in climate, these edge species will provide the means by which the environment will establish a new equilibrium.

This is a simplification of a long process, but the point cannot be put too simply: change, meaningful change, almost always comes from the edge, the margins. Our economy is no different: economic innovation usually comes from the margins of the culture. I call this entrepreneurial growth "internal differentiation." MIT researcher David Birch calls it "atomization." While the *Fortune* 500 companies battle it out in the tough international markets of oil, steel, cars, and computers—a process that should make the companies leaner and more competitive—the "understory" of American business is being "infilled" by millions of spinoffs, home-grown businesses, cottage industries, service companies, small stores, design firms, and contract manufacturers.

This adaptive, questing, continuous reexamination is exactly how the economy and the culture try to maintain their health. This is the precise reason there will always be new, small businesses. Because big business depends on stability and uniformity, while small business thrives on change and difference, it may be that, in this rapidly changing world, the big businesses can learn from the small ones.

CONSUMERS ARE BECOMING CUSTOMERS

Before World War II we were customers, patrons, clientele. In the new era of mass manufacturing and marketing policies after the war, we were *consumers,* and in the subservient role that word implies we helped sustain the longest period of economic growth the world has seen in one country. Because of its enviable and quasi-monopolistic position as "supplier to the world," American business forgot about people. The customer was neglected in the surge of growth and expansion that lasted until the early 1970s. Market share was sought through advertising, not innovation.

It was a curious time because, for many reasons, it did not make sense for the individual to buy the best product. Real wages were rising so fast in this period, with the real cost of goods declining accordingly, that it was cheaper to replace the washing machine or lawn mower after five years than it was to fix it.

So we consumed. To "consume" means to use up, to waste, to destroy. The word has the same root as the disease "consumption." By no coincidence we became, in Vance Packard's famous words, "the waste makers."

This state of affairs is changing, and the pressure for change is coming from the "bottom," the customers, not from the top. In today's economy, consumption is no longer rewarded. Real income has fallen in the past five, ten, fifteen years, any way you wish to measure it. In response, we could "buy down"—buy cheaper goods to compensate for lowered income—but instead North Americans are buying up. Because of the pressure on our real income, we have become very value and quality conscious. We cannot afford to be mere consumers. We buy products that work better and last longer. We are spending our money as the Europeans, even the Japanese, always have, and it should be no surprise that we often prefer their products to our own. We have raised the stakes. It is our demand for a better designed and operated world that is behind the tumultuous change we see in the marketplace today.

We want to do business with companies that back their products and take care of the needs of their customers *after* the transaction, as well as before. To be a customer means to become *accustomed*, to be in the habit of doing something. In this new economy, we want to develop patterns of patronage that will reward us. Service is information, too— very powerful information. It tells us everything about a company's attitude toward us. We prefer a relationship with a business that won't punish us if something should go wrong with a product, that gives us a sense of well-being, that builds over time.

Stories we hear about how a customer was treated by a company are clear signals how to spend our money. When we hear from an ex-director of General Motors, H. Ross Perot, that a Toyota dealer selling 2,500 cars a year requires twenty service bays to take care of its customers, whereas a Cadillac dealer selling the same number of cars requires 110 service bays working two shifts, we get the message. When we read and hear about Audi at first refusing to recall its cars, many of whose owners reported a problem of sudden acceleration, we get the message. When we hear that Nordstrom, the West Coast department store, has a cheerful no-questions-asked policy on returns, we get the message.

We seek out good companies to patronize because we can no longer afford to be taken for granted. Therefore, the small business is in the catbird seat. Quality and service are its specialty.

4

If It's a Good Idea, It's Too Late

I'M NOT sure when I got the first glimmer of the idea for the mail order tool company, Smith & Hawken. I suppose it was one cold and blustery day on the high prairie of the Texas panhandle—in 1972, when I was still in the food business. I had forty thousand acres of land under contract on fifty-eight different farms in thirty-seven states. One of my jobs was to inspect crops, make sure that good agricultural practices were employed, negotiate agreements, and generally keep in touch with the all-important supplier. On that March day in Texas, I was at Carl Wheeler's farm to see how much moisture the winter wheat had received. Carl and I walked the fences and studied the uniform rows of tiny sprouts. He had grabbed a shovel to use as a walking stick, and occasionally he turned the soil to look for signs of water. Dry land farming in that part of the country is risky, and the wheat looked poor that year. Every dry spadeful confirmed our doubts about the crop. When we returned to Carl's pickup he tossed the shovel into the bed. I noticed a bunch of other tools lying there, most of them with broken handles or split blades. He saw me looking at that graveyard and muttered something about fixing them one day, and then he added that he wouldn't have to if American companies still made good tools.

On the trip back to Amarillo I was treated to a forty-minute lecture on the degeneration of the American tool business since World War II. Carl knew the dates, mergers, buyouts. He had thought about this for years. His last line stuck fast in my mind: "I don't know why those companies take us for fools."

When we got out of the truck I looked more closely at the pile of damaged goods: rakes, hoes, a lot of shovels, and a posthole digger. Handles were broken well up the shaft. That meant the wood was poorly selected first-growth ash. Tanged hoes had been torn away from the ferrule. The shovels had snapped at just about every point from the handle to the socket to the head. The teeth of the rakes were splayed in several directions. The blade of the posthole digger had crumpled on one side, probably after striking a rock.

Two years later I was in England, touring British estate gardens and arboretums. That environment was as rich and verdant as the Texas panhandle had been marginal and dry.

The gardens were splendid and the craft of gardening was more highly developed than any I had ever seen, even in Japan. As I watched the gardeners work I studied their tools. I hefted a spade, the tool of choice. It seemed unusually heavy and it was sharp as an ax, shiny with the patina of constant use. The gardener saw me looking at it and came over to discuss its merits.

That was not merely a spade, that was *his* spade. He had owned it for twenty years. I asked him if it wasn't heavy and tiring to use. With a smile he invited me to give it a try, continuing the trench he was digging. I toiled away as he grew increasingly amused. In his Lancashire accent he said, "Let your tool do the work. That's what it's made for." He showed me how to use the weight of the spade, how to make the tool an extension of my arms, how to move my body. He took his tools to the job just as a carpenter would. He purchased his tools from the same ironmonger his father had patronized. This gardener had studied his craft in a Lancashire college for four years, apprenticed for many more, and only now, in his fifties, did he consider himself knowledgeable of his subject in any meaningful way. Nobody takes the English gardener for a fool.

When I returned to the States, I suggested to several companies that they import the excellent English tools. I didn't think it was a big business, but it seemed like an obvious business for someone. Surely professional gardeners here would value quality implements as much as their English counterparts. No one was interested. I turned back to writing and forgot the matter.

I couldn't write all the time, however. My recreation was gardening. After that trip to England, I couldn't browse in the hardware store or look into my toolshed at the bent trowel without thinking that it didn't have to be this way. In 1978 I joined the board of Ecology Action, a local nonprofit group in Palo Alto, California, which initiated the first curbside recycling program in the United States. Ecology Action was also deeply interested in gardening and operated a five-acre test plot on land donated by Syntex, the pharmaceutical firm. They were researching high-yield methods of agriculture that didn't rely on artificial fertilizers and expensive chemicals. The goal was to develop a method that could be exported to Third World countries in order to raise the nutritional intake of vitamins and minerals.

The leaders of the program, John and Betsy Jeavons and Robin Leler, had opened a small store near Stanford University to support their work. They sold seeds, books, and, to my great surprise, the best English professional garden tools.

Shortly after I joined the board the supply of tools was cut off. The American distributor had gone out of business for the strangest of reasons. The outfit was located near a flood-prone area of the Ohio River. In one flood the entire inventory of English tools was submerged and allowed to float around for several days. When the waters receded, the company dried out the tools and sold them. Naturally they rusted from the inside out, their customers complained, business dried up, distribution ceased.

Ecology Action needed a supplier, so I offered to set up a small import business as part of the operations. I wrote to the Bulldog Tool Company, declared our interest in their tools, and waited. Months went by and I wrote again.

More months went by and I more or less forgot about tools for a second time. Why should the English be interested? We were a small, almost inconsequential educational foundation that had written to them on plain stationery with no letterhead.

After nine months the reply came. Ian Hall, a data processing technician from the parent company, had been appointed as the new export manager of the tool company. On the day he arrived, he noticed our latest letter about to be thrown into the circular file by the outgoing manager. "Another one of those inquiries from stateside," the departing manager said. "We don't answer them anymore because the U.S. has been such a bother." Indeed it had been. The distributor on the Ohio River had gone out of business and tarnished the reputation of the tools in the process. The previous distributor had gone out of business, too. The English firm had lost over $150,000 on bad debts, and they had been sued for trademark infringement by another U.S. company.

Nevertheless, Ian Hall retrieved my letter and answered it. He checked our background and references. It appeared we would be in business after all. The problem was that I didn't want to be in business full time. I wanted to write, too. So I found a partner, Dave Smith, the manager of a cooperative food market and one of the best "people" people I have ever encountered.

What would we call this nonprofit company? Fundamental Tools? English Tools? Basic Tools? Real Good Tools? Intensive Tools? We didn't like any of these options, but the lack of a name soon became the least of our problems. Our lawyer said that unless we became a for-profit enterprise the tax-exempt status of Ecology Action would be jeopardized. But John Jeavons said no to that idea. He didn't want anyone to think that Ecology Action benefited from its activities, and he had a point. Ecology Action was a teaching and research organization, and John, with his academic background, bridled at any hint of conflict or personal profit.

By this time, several months after first hearing from Ian Hall, the tools were already ordered and were on their way whether we were ready for them or not. Dave Smith and I didn't want to renege on our order—the English had a bad enough impression of American business practices—so it looked as if we'd have to go into a regular business, complete with shareholders, capital, and an official plan. This was not at all what we had had in mind.

Nobody wanted to own the company. John and Betsy Jeavons, still concerned about any hint of impropriety in the relationship between this nameless orphan of a company and Ecology Action, wouldn't accept a single share of stock. Nobody, literally, wanted to own the company and I had visions of the Bulldog Tool Company being burned again—another load of tools shipped to their third soon-to-be-defunct American distributor. That night I took a five-hour bath as my wife Anna brought in steaming tea kettles after the hot water heater had run out. I tried to soak myself out of this dilemma. In the end the conclusion was simple. Dave Smith and I had given our word to the English suppliers, so we would form a company. We needed a name, so we gave it our own WASPy surnames, Smith and Hawken.

I balked when Smith & Hawken was gearing up because

I was writing at the time but, going all the way back to that day in the Texas panhandle, tools have always been a major interest in my life. Tools and gardening and agriculture. The company was almost a decade in the conception. The other businesses I've been associated with have started in equally strange and convoluted ways. Each has risen from deep within my own life and experience, yet it wasn't something "driving" me. A successful business *pulls* you toward it. I'm slow on the uptake and I have to let a situation sink in for some time before I feel that I have grasped it. I'm not arguing that this lumbering gait is the only way to start a business, but I am suggesting that your best idea for a business will be something that is deep within you, something that can't be stolen because it is uniquely yours, and anyone else trying to execute it without the (perhaps unconscious) thought you have given the subject will fail. It's not basically different from writing a novel. A good business and a good novel are faithful and uncluttered expressions of yourself.

Likewise, the business that you can succeed in is intricately woven into your existence, so much so that it may be invisible right now. Your business must be an extension of who you are and what you are trying to learn and achieve. You know that you want to replace, improve, or change. Begin where the tool breaks, the service slips, or the shoe pinches.

Yvon Chouinard started Patagonia, the purveyor of climbing equipment and outdoor clothing, as a one-man enterprise in Ventura, California, in 1958. Chouinard wanted to replace the imported soft iron pitons that lasted only one or two climbs with "chrome mollies" (chromium-molybdenum steel) that were harder, stronger, and longer lasting. Chouinard started Patagonia with no plan, management experience, advertising, or expertise in forging. He worked in a shed with a hand forge with $800 of capital borrowed from his mother. What Chouinard did have was a knowledge of the equipment he needed in his own climbs, and a sense that the serious climbing world would follow his lead. The idea was right under every mountain climber's nose. Only Chouinard sniffed it out. Today, Patagonia makes twenty-five hundred products and grosses $50 million.

The great value and weight of a sound business idea are not in the conclusion—"I will start a piton company"—but in the complex processes that lead to that final enunciation. The idea itself is just the tip of the iceberg. The iceberg is your life. Don't worry about anyone stealing your idea, because they can't steal your life. I have a friend who almost every time I see him prefaces his new idea with the admonition, "Now you must not tell anyone." He needn't worry.

One of my favorite business start-up stories is the unlikely tale of Ben Cohen and Jerry Greenfield. Ben and Jerry met at the tail of the pack in seventh-grade track, when they discovered that their love of food placed them at a serious disadvantage in gym class. They loped behind their classmates and talked about what did interest them. Years later, after careers in social work and academia, Ben and Jerry decided to pursue their lifelong love of food in a business. After looking at equipment costs, they narrowed the field to bagels and ice cream. Because bagel machinery cost slightly more, they chose ice cream and sent $5 to Penn State for a correspondence course in making it. Since the course used the "open text" method of testing, the two students looked up the answers to the questions, got 100 percent on every test, and passed in fine flavor.

Ben believed that college towns with warm climates were the best market for ice cream. He and Jerry purchased an atlas, studied the country, and visited prospective towns. Sure enough, the warmer the town, the more ice cream shops there were. The market was crowded. Too crowded, so they went north instead, to Burlington, Vermont, where there wasn't a single Baskin Robbins outlet. Ben and Jerry scraped together $8,000 and opened an ice cream stand in an abandoned gas station with low rent.

That was 1978 and business was great—until winter. Their only hope of surviving was to package their premium ice cream and sell it wholesale. Their creative flavors have made Ben & Jerry's a $27 million company with national distribution.

A business idea is not about opportunism. The real estate broker who learns clandestinely that the new airport will be built to the southwest of town and buys up property there is "doing business," but he is not operating with a business idea. There is no imagination involved in this business. Many financial dealings depend on secrecy in order for them to be profitable. A large area of American business involving finance, investment and merchant banking, real estate, and other financial services operates, at least initially, clandestinely and confidentially. Economist Robert Reich calls this activity "paper entrepreneurship." It is also referred to as the second, the phantom, and the meta-economy. Whatever its name, it can be distinguished from a creative business idea by one factor. It does not create new products, new value, or real economic growth. In "paper entrepreneurship" the answer to why a person is "in business" is always the same: to make money. These transactions merely rearrange the deck chairs and, if our society becomes too obsessed with such legerdemain, we may well go under as a vital economic system. We have all read about the current crop of M.B.A. students, many of whom are headed for Wall Street. Few express an interest in manufacturing, and this attitude is looked at with alarm by social theorists. I don't believe it matters. There will always be the Yvon Chouinards, Ben Cohens, and Jerry Greenfields.

Good ideas often do not look very good at first or even second glance, but don't worry if your business idea sounds weird, crazy, or obscure. Like a puppy, many good ideas are awkward, helpless, and unimpressive. George Gilder, author of *The Spirit of Enterprise*, wrote, "It is the entrepreneurs who know the rules of the world and the laws of God." Even though we want our entrepreneurial heroes to experience epiphanous moments of inspiration, it is hardly so. The idea for a business is usually the result of a fascination, preoccupation, or even obsession with some mundane field or pursuit. You mull the notion, free-associate, delve, and tinker late into the night. Ray Kroc, the founder of McDonald's Corporation, discovered the future of American fast food at a hamburger stand that was his best customer for the milk shake blenders he was selling at the time. To find out why this hamburger place belonging to the McDonald brothers was the most popular in southern California, Kroc hung out in the parking lot with the teenagers.

Certainly one of the more famous heroes of American business in the 1980s is Steven Jobs of Apple Computer. But a close inspection of the early days at Apple does not reveal two boy geniuses (Jobs along with Stephen Wozniak) huddled in Jobs' parents' garage inventing the first home computer. Jobs, who had been bouncing from company to company, from India to a commune in Oregon, was not getting along with his colleagues at Atari, and he had not endeared himself in Silicon Valley with his personality. Wozniak was working at Hewlett-Packard Co. and had spent months trying to give away the schematics to the home computer he had designed. It never had occurred to him to sell the completed machine.

Geniuses they may be, but Jobs and Wozniak didn't set up shop to build computers. Their first idea was to sell circuit boards made of commonly available parts so that hackers could build their own computers. Wozniak had been designing boards and giving away the schematics. Jobs had a better idea: sell the boards.

With the hope of selling one hundred boards, they called on Paul Terrell, a friend who had just opened one of the first computer stores, the Byte Shop in Mountain View, California. Terrell wasn't interested in selling the boards but he told Jobs that he would buy fifty fully assembled computers, made from the boards, to sell for between $500 and $600. Jobs delivered the machines but they didn't sell well. During this slow period, he agonized over his future in business and seriously considered studying Buddhism at a Japanese monastery. He wasn't even sure he wanted to go into business.

Good ideas rarely start out that way. If you believe you

have a good one, try it out on friends. If they say you have a wonderful idea, you may be in trouble: an idea everyone recognizes as great has probably arrived on the scene too late. But if your friends look confused and shrug their shoulders, things are looking up. If they snicker and guffaw, you may be on to something. At least your idea is new. It may defy common sense or the logic of the market as it now exists, but it may also be breaking new ground or reassessing the given. Thus the initial hesitation in the marketplace in reaction to Apple's first computers.

However, ideas that are too original can also be difficult to execute. They may be you, but you may be so far ahead of the market that you end up doing research and development for the people who come behind you. This may have been the case with the Alto computer at Xerox PARC. Who can say whether Xerox's personal computer would have been accepted in 1975? Maybe that would have been a few years too early—we will never know. Being first in a market can be a decisive advantage or it can put you out there too early.

The groundbreaking business idea that can also be a success is the one that's right under your nose, probably sitting around the house, office, garage, or yard. It's there but the rest of us are not aware of it. You'll find yourself worrying it like a bone. You will begin to see the world from the perspective of your idea. If you start a small brewery like Old New York Brewing Co. in New York City, or Granville Brewery in Vancouver, you will have begun to notice beer years before you go into business. You'll learn the taste, the label, the importer, and the market for dozens, hundreds, of beers. You'll ask friends about their favorite brews. Market research of a sort, but visceral and subjective. You'll slowly find yourself becoming that new idea.

Matthew Reich, the founder of Old New York Brewing Co., maker of New Amsterdam beer, did just that, but he was a wine expert before he was a beer expert. He would have gone into the wine business but he wanted to live and work in New York, and he decided that premium beer, as opposed to yet another winemaking operation, was a more likely venture on the East Coast. After he made this decision, he started studying beer with the diligence he had given to wine. He took classes at the Center for Brewing Studies in San Francisco. He did research with a brewmaster. Only after two years of this informal research did he begin to gear up for the big push.

You will be your business long before you open the doors. If big companies could do research any better than you can, why is it that the food companies launch several thousand new products every year, of which only a tiny fraction successfully compete in the supermarket? If you have a food passion and can't satisfy it, you have a better chance than General Foods.

There are ample opportunities. The American consumer is inherently dissatisfied. My businesses have started from my being a customer and not liking what I could buy. I suspect your business will begin that way, too.

Remember that in business you are never trying to "beat" the competition. You are trying to give your customer something other than what they are receiving from the competition. It is a waste of time and energy trying to beat the competition because the customer doesn't care about that rivalry. This is why Carl Schmitt, founder of the University National Bank & Trust Company in Palo Alto, California, has never bothered to go around meeting the other bankers in town, normal procedure for many new bankers. Schmitt's energy is directed to the customers.

Your business is not only close to you, it is also close to your customer. It follows that you must be very careful entering a market that's fat and happy. In my town, which is not growing at all, there are three strong food markets— a Safeway, an independent, and a smaller, but full-service, specialty market. Each store is good and well liked. Most of my friends shop at all three. Attempts by other companies to get into the food business in my town have failed. The next attempt will probably fail, too.

You will not be able to conquer the market. Don't get suckered into an idea that is the commercial equivalent of the charge of the light brigade. Besides, what people want is not that tough a sale. A good idea will not require exhortations from the bully pulpit, hucksterism, sales pyramids, and cheerleaders. A business that depends on these techniques is not a business worth owning. Good business ideas provide people with something that was right there—or not right there—all the time, but no one recognized it. When you do recognize it and provide it, they'll buy it.

Another caution: Don't start two businesses. One idea is sufficient, and bringing it to commercial fruition is hard enough. The world gives you permission to do, or try to do, one thing well. If you do that well, you get permission to move on to the next thing. That's how we learn as children. That's how businesses grow. The person who wants to write novels and print them on her own letterpress is starting two businesses. The person who buys a farm to raise beef and at the same time opens a butcher shop is starting two businesses. He would have a much better chance of survival if he got the farm on a steady footing before venturing into the retail business.

I have a friend who is a marine biologist, a good sailor, and a fine ecologist. He had been in academia most of his life before he came to me with a business plan. He had designed a lightweight, fairly inexpensive boat that would be a seafaring freighter powered by sails. The boat had an innovative hull and sail design that would allow it to travel worldwide, beyond the restrictions usually imposed on sailing craft by the prevailing trade winds. Further, he envisioned this boat collecting marine algae and plankton growing in the more remote parts of the oceans and processing them for use in pharmaceuticals. Fish caught at sea would be iced down and sold wholesale. And finally, the boat would have a smaller' sister that could be operated by the coast-dwelling residents of poor countries, who could augment their diets with fish and also have a source of revenue.

This plan contained at least six businesses: designing boats, constructing boats, hauling freight, harvesting pharmaceuticals, selling fish, and marketing small fishing vessels in Third World countries. And each of these businesses was highly experimental and innovative. This was a great plan except for its impossibility. Despite great personal effort, the business (or businesses) never got off the ground.

Even an established company must be careful about doing two things at once. (Conglomerates are learning this lesson every day: W. R. Grace, the specialty chemical giant, went into restaurants, the oil business, and sporting goods in a big way. All of those businesses have either been sold or are on the block.) When we started our catalog business at Smith & Hawken, we were deluged with requests from companies that wanted to purchase from us wholesale. Because we needed the cash, we succumbed. But we quickly pulled back and have never sold wholesale again, for two reasons.

First, customers ordering from a catalog want something unique (we are the sole American distributor for many of our products). Generally speaking, if customers can get a product locally, they don't order from a catalog. (Patagonia is an exception in this regard. Almost all of the items in their catalog are available in retail stores, but no retail account carries all their items.)

Second, our business was based on service. We wanted direct contact with our customers in order to satisfy them completely. We could not control what happened when our products were sold through a retailer.

I am not saying that businesses cannot change their purpose from time to time. They certainly can. Retailers change into wholesalers, manufacturers turn into retailers, service companies start selling products, and so on. But you can make these difficult transitions only if the market is willing and if you move from a successful base. Permission in the marketplace is a delicate bond and agreement, and it should never be taken for granted. It is hard to forge but easy to break.

Many business ideas are duds. While you might have a great idea every seven days or seven years, the rest of the world is relentlessly probing every corner of commerce and service to figure out how to make a successful business. Here are some ways of looking at the world with an eye to creating a new business from an old one or enhancing an ordinary business into a better one.

RE-CREATE SOMETHING THAT HAS BEEN LOST

I was recently asked by a reporter what business I would start today and I said a bank. I don't know about you, but I can't find a large bank with the full range of services whose tellers last more than three months, or one that really "trusts" me rather than merely has the word in its name.

Seven years ago, Carl Schmitt opened University National Bank in Palo Alto. In order to open an account at UNB, a potential depositor must be recommended by a customer of the bank. Otherwise, he must submit to an extensive credit check. But once you're in, you're trusted. You are much more likely to receive a phone call rather than an overdrawn charge if you bounce a check. The pens on the tables aren't chained down. Free shoeshines and nice restrooms are available in the lobby. Walla Walla sweet onions are available free to every customer in the summer, and the customers are notified by phone when the shipment is in. The staff knows the customers—and the customers know the names of the tellers, and bring them gifts and do favors for them. Staff turnover at UNB is negligible.

Carl Schmitt didn't create anything new. He re-created

something that had been lost: a bank where they know you.

The first time I articulated a plan for Smith & Hawken it sounded like this: "We're going to sell hand-forged, short-handled, English-style spades and forks to the North American gardener who is unfamiliar with such tools through a direct mail catalog because the distribution system normally used by the hardware/nursery business is too costly and inefficient."

Americans didn't use forks and spades in their gardens. They preferred shovels. Our tools were short-handled but Americans preferred long-handled. Americans had become accustomed to low-priced, mass-produced tools with a short life. Ours lasted for a lifetime.

There was not a shred of evidence to support this plan. I couldn't begin to prove that Smith & Hawken was possible, much less growable. On the contrary, the two previous distributors of these tools had gone out of business. The line itself, named Bulldog, had lost a trademark lawsuit to a firm that had no intention of using the name of which it was the lawful owner. Most important of all, there was no evidence that American gardeners were interested in English tools. Wilkinson, Spear & Jackson, Jenks & Cattell, and Stanley of England had all tried to penetrate the North American market and failed. One of them had even set up a warehouse over here, and another had purchased an American garden tool company. All to no avail.

No company had successfully sold garden equipment in a mail order catalog. The only successful catalogs in the genre were in the seed, bulb, and plant nursery business. Why would people buy tools through the mail that they were used to buying at the hardware store or garden center? People like to heft and feel tools before purchasing them.

Just as a market survey probably would have confirmed the decision of Xerox executives to ignore the home computer market, so would my market survey have instructed me to go back to writing for a living. Luckily, I couldn't afford the survey. Smith & Hawken grew because it had at its roots a sense of what was lost. Good tools had always been a part of American life from frontier days until World War II. What had been lost was still needed.

ENHANCE THE COMMONPLACE

Take a prosaic, everyday, kick-around sort of product and make it real again. Hamburgers, for example. There are so many bad hamburgers in this world I venture to say that anyone with a hot grill who makes an honest one with generous portions and fresh fried onions will never lack for customers. In other words, take a product and reduce it to its essence.

In the mid-seventies I was hired as a consultant by Lazzari Fuel Co. in San Francisco, which was struggling to develop a market for its mesquite charcoal, which they were selling as a fuel. But mesquite is more than a fuel. It burns at 1,700 degrees, instead of the 700 degrees generated by standard charcoal briquets, and sears meat quickly, locking in the flavor as well as adding its own unique flavor. I suggested that Lazzari differentiate its product from the commonplace by changing the packaging, and selling mesquite as an *ingredient*, not a fuel. They were the first

73

mesquite purveyor in the United States to adopt this course. Business soared.

Korean immigrants took over the corner vegetable store business in New York City because the other vendors had become lazy. The Koreans restored the corner store to a place where you could actually shop for fresh produce attractively displayed, at affordable prices with good quality. The success of the sundry fresh cookie companies was mainly because there wasn't a good cookie in sight—in bakeries, stores, or supermarkets—before the David Liedermans and Debbi Fieldses greased their tins.

In the case of Smith & Hawken, all the early products we sold were so exceedingly commonplace they were ignored and unattended to by vendors and manufacturers. Hand tools are a dead market, not growing at all. We noticed that hand tools such as forks, spades, and trowels were so prosaic that people were beginning not even to understand them. So we began to inform them about style, weight, design, and usage. Our catalogs described how they were invented and by whom—easy to do because our vendor in England literally invented the steel fork and spade. We believed that if we could present a sufficient amount of information that was compelling and interesting in its own right, we could get people interested in the differences and advantages of our tools.

RAISE THE ANTE

When going into a business, never just meet the competition. Examine a product or business closely and make a detailed list of all the qualities that could improve it in your customer's eyes. Every year the stakes get higher in business, so you want to be the person who sets the stakes, not plays catch-up. If you start a business behind the competition, most of your effort will be directed toward reacting to what it does. If you go your own way, set the standards, and keep looking forward, the majority of your creative energy goes into the ideas that promote new growth.

You see countless examples of how the ante is being raised in everyday life. In the restaurant business, the food today has to be fresh—not frozen, microwaved, or pre-cooked. In mail order, it is hard to establish a company without having an "800" phone number. Domino's Pizza raised the ante in my town by offering home delivery. Now, just about every pizza place in the neighborhood delivers.

Smith & Hawken raised the ante initially with our guarantee. The fact that our tools are 20 to 30 percent more expensive no longer looks like a cost but an investment because conventional tools wear out so quickly. Hand tools are something of a throwaway item in this culture, with little or no warranty in terms of product life or quality. We back ours for life. By backing our tools unconditionally, we became the low-cost provider.

We have also tried to raise the ante by service. Knowing that we are competing not only with other catalogs but with local hardware stores, we try to offer better service than they can. We send out all orders within twenty-four hours, deliver to the customer's door, and pick up at the same door if there's a problem.

REVEAL A BUSINESS WITHIN
A BUSINESS

Look for two related businesses that can better be done when one is removed. Twenty years ago, cookware was sold in the hardware stores and department stores. It took Chuck Williams of Williams-Sonoma to do it right. He started with a hardware store that sold good cookware and finally ended up taking all the hardware out and leaving the cookware. There are now many imitators but Williams-Sonoma is the acknowledged leader.

We did the same thing at Smith & Hawken. Nurseries did not see tools, implements, books, and ornaments as an important business. Particularly in the last few years, nurseries have turned to a fast-food frame of mind, emphasizing "color" in the form of annuals which have to be replaced every year. The durable side of the nursery business was treated as an afterthought. There was little effort at merchandising and scant information or advice was provided.

Our business took the ugly duckling of the nursery business and made it interesting. We traveled to a dozen countries tracking down tools, terra-cotta, books, instruments, machinery, and devices that would make a garden more enjoyable, easy to work within, or more pleasing to the eye. And, of course, we get hundreds of requests every year from nurseries that want to buy from us wholesale.

RESTORE A BUSINESS

Sometimes business segments begin to separate as if they were parts of an old house. This happens because the particular type of business is seen as mature, with no prospects for growth. It can also happen when a business is shunted to the side by large national chains or discounters, or when a product line is seen as too commonplace or ordinary. Diners and drive-ins were almost anachronistic in the sixties and seventies, pushed aside by the onslaught of fast-food chains and convenience foods. Now they are being revived, complete with carhops, shiny chromium jukeboxes at the table, thick shakes, and double fries. I am convinced that an old-fashioned, full-service hardware store would do very well in some towns and in locations situated near boatyards or where there are old houses—where people work with their hands. The Old New York Brewing Co. is putting restaurants in its breweries, a practice hundreds of years old in England and Germany.

In one of our Smith & Hawken retail stores we are slowly trying to re-create a full-service nursery. It will probably take years to do since the world of plants is so complex, but rather than buy from the large growers and distributors, we have tediously sought out our own small growers to produce healthy specimens that have been shunted aside by modernity and convenience—old fragrant roses, sweet-scented clematis, full arrays of lavender, and the like. In the process we are educating both ourselves and the customer, slowly changing people's orientation in gardening from annuals and bright color toward long-lived perennials and landscapes that blend and work together in subtler ways. That business harks back to nineteenth-century England, and it is timeless in appeal.

BE THE MOST COMPLETE

Take any business—pet shop, flower store, window washer, or bicycle shop—and make yours the most thorough, best inventoried, highest profile sort of business in its area. Become the arbiter by which other competing businesses are measured. When Ford ran ads that said their car was as quiet as a Mercedes-Benz, they merely pointed to the most complete car made. Don't live up to a criterion, set it. You can do this with a product by designing it better, presenting it better, giving better instructions, and supplying better after-market support. When customers buy bulbs from Burpee's, they receive only a depth chart. When they buy from White Flower Farm, they get plant markers and a complete cultural manual.

In 1981, Smith & Hawken discovered a German watering system made of high-impact plastics that connects with snaps rather than the usual threading. It was fast, efficient, innovative. Although the individual parts worked well as components, they worked better together. Believing that the customer should have access to all of the products because they were designed as a system, we picked up the entire line and put it in our catalog, devoting many pages to it. Other companies picked up one or two of the top-selling items.

Our two biggest catalog competitors told the German vendor we were crazy to sell the full line. From their point of view, every item in a catalog has to "make its space"— pay its own way. Spare parts, O-rings, advice, and the usual watering components do not, by definition, pay their way. Then the vendor started to sell the products to any and all comers, from K mart to Sears, which took only the high-turnover items. A strange thing happened. The better everyone else did with the high-turnover pieces of the system, the better we did, because we were the only company that carried the full line. Despite competing with the national chains, we are still the top retailer of the product in the United States—all because we chose to give our customers a complete selection. If we had "creamed" the line, we would have been competing with K mart.

BE THE LOW-COST PROVIDER

Buy as directly as possible, sell as directly as possible, and reduce overhead as much as possible. Then get out of the way, for if you have done it right, you will be mobbed. This trend is seen in the spread of warehouse stores on the West Coast, one-hundred-thousand-square-foot emporiums that are basically materials-handling warehouses in which consumers buy at cost plus 12 percent. For many small retail stores, it is cheaper to buy at these stores than from a distributor. A warehouse store business can do in excess of $100 million a year at a single location.

You don't have to be large to do it. Smith & Hawken sells items that are not, with few exceptions, commonly available. Yet we do have our competitors and we deal with them by underpricing them. With only one exception, we do not buy from middlemen. We buy only from the maker. To sell the best, you have to buy the best. This requires being alert, aggressive, and vigorous in your buying activity.

"BEING" RATHER THAN "DOING"

Royal Dutch Shell recently undertook a study on business longevity. That company wanted to find out why some companies had endured for centuries, especially when their purpose or main business had changed or been yanked from under them by external events. Shell had good reason to study these companies. The world's second-largest oil company doesn't think any company will be in the oil business a hundred years from now.

The study concluded that these venerable companies had a charismatic leader, usually the founder, who had made a lasting impression and established a guiding ethic for all who followed. Another conclusion, and related to the first one, was that these companies survived the upheavals of the marketplace and the world-at-large because they had "being" goals instead of "doing" goals. Their business was centered on a way of interacting with the world, not on providing one specific product or service.

A goal for a new diaper company might be "providing the whitest diapers in America." That's laudable, but a better goal would be "providing the greatest assistance to mothers of newborns." A company with that second attitude will have less of a problem changing products when the country switches to Ultra Pampers.

If your company is Bio-Bottoms and you are mothers who are dedicated to making mothering and parenting more intelligent, delightful, and rewarding, your future is virtually unlimited. You will always have a purpose and an agenda to guide you, and the world will always need your company. You will have a rich array of possibilities to choose from. Such businesses are not easily toppled by temporary success or failure.

MAKE IT FUN

People are a wee bit uptight when they spend their money. When the packaging, service, or retail ambience conveys a sense of esprit, humor, and high spirits people will stay around and support that operation. Increasingly, people go to stores in order to "be" there, and then and only then do they spend money. Retailing is becoming part entertainment, part showmanship, and part provision of goods. No store understands this better than Banana Republic, the successful retailer of "safari" and travel clothing. Every last detail of the decor, music, signs, and merchandise evokes a different time and place.

I don't believe there is a business in America that would not benefit by loosening up and having fun with its customers. Laughter and delight bond the customer to the company because they build trust and rapport. By tradition, no business is more staid than a bank, but Carl Schmitt's bank in Palo Alto sets a different tone with a painting on the side of the building showing an alien emerging from a flying saucer that crashed into the bank. The back windows of the four bank vans show the following scenes going on "inside" the trucks: two convicts playing cards; two masked men cracking a vault (painted on the side of that van is a policeman waiting inside to catch them); two counterfeiters inspecting their newest fortune; and a washing machine out of which is bubbling a pile of bills—

laundered money. People enjoy the art and remember the bank.

If you aren't having some fun, you might wonder just what you are doing in your business life. Laughter and good humor are the canaries in the mine of commerce. If employees, customers, and vendors don't laugh and have a good time at your company, something is wrong.

5

The Art of the Incremental

FIVE YEARS ago, a group of retailers opened a new store in the Stanford Shopping Center in Palo Alto, California, after raising large amounts of capital with a good business plan. Their idea was a West Coast version of Brookstone, the New Hampshire merchandiser of hard-to-find hand tools. The store was a big success and this first bloom of prosperity kicked off the opening of three more stores in other shopping centers in California. The additional stores struggled and lost money, and the company was disposed of by the original owners—experienced retailers all.

Having opened one successful store, they thought that

all of the original assumptions of their business plan had been confirmed. After the three flops, none of them were. These businesspeople forgot one major fact. The Stanford Shopping Center, located within half an hour's drive of Silicon Valley and the southern suburbs of San Francisco, is one of the most successful shopping centers in the world. It is so packed with people willing to be parted from their money that stores will do anything in order to get in. The worst corner space is a bonanza. A success at Stanford Shopping Center does not necessarily indicate the inherent soundness of a business idea. So the business plan for the California store wasn't such a good one, after all, because it wasn't complete.

After you have your business idea, I recommend that you subject it to the scrutiny of a business plan, for two good reasons. One is to create a tool that will help you conduct your business. The second is to create a way to secure capital.

The moment I write this I have to state that many of the spectacular business successes in the past ten years, especially those outside the areas of technology and manufacturing, which require large amounts of capital and therefore a good plan to attract that capital, were started by the seat of someone's pants. Patagonia, Apple Computer, and Esprit, to name three, began without a business plan or any other type of financing document, or any written description or strategy. This is the bootstrap method of starting a business, the style often synonymous with the entrepreneur, a kind of shoot-from-the-hip product slinger who takes his or her chances in the marketplace. I will talk about bootstrapping operations in detail in a later chapter, but the point now is that while bootstrapping apparently lacks planning, there *is* a planning process going on. Many market-wise entrepreneurs just cannot articulate in an understandable fashion what they are doing. They are not thinking verbally, but visually, spatially, or in some other fashion. They can recognize the rationality of what they do only in retrospect. Often, this type of person eventually stops trying to communicate because he or she is not understood. But this does not mean the person is not planning. The plan may be totally different from the conventional planning process, and so deeply internalized that there is very little plan showing for outsiders to follow.

The flagrantly successful bootstrap companies were direct extensions of the personalities of their energetic and spirited founders, whose dynamic styles played such an important role in the successful founding of these new businesses. But for every Patagonia, how many other good business ideas foundered for lack of a clear program that could guide their growth? A lot, including the Brookstone look-alike.

A business plan broadly describes the nature of the business, the type of product being manufactured or service offered, and the advantage or benefits the product offers. The plan is specific regarding ways of getting the product to market, an analysis of the competition, financial projections stretching out for five years (usually long enough so they are meaningless), and short biographies of the principals. A business plan is a test of the depth and thoroughness with which you have thought out your idea. The act of looking ahead to the possibilities and problems of your business will provide guidance and help prevent mistakes. Later in this chapter, I provide specific notes on writing your business plan. First, these more general considerations to keep in mind as you plan your business.

DON'T PLAN SOMEONE ELSE'S BUSINESS

As the initiator of a new business, you should be willing to take perceived risks. But those who place money into your company have a responsibility to see these risks minimized. When describing your business, you will need to reconcile these opposing requirements. The temptation is to fudge your plan toward what you believe the reader wants to read, rather than what you want to do. If your choice is between getting funding for the compromised business that your capital partners want to see, and not getting funded at all, I recommend not getting funded at all.

Certainly the biggest lie forced by potential investors on new companies is the "growth rate." Because venture capitalists do take risk, and because two out of three of their investments fail or never go anywhere, the third business has to make up for the other two. To do so, it must return at least 40 to 80 percent per year on invested capital. This rate of growth is acceptable for some companies, but in other cases it is distorting and destructive.

You cannot secure adequate capital funding if you present a business plan that says you are going to grow only 20 percent a year for the next seven years. Your objective is to be sure that your interests and those of your investors are aligned, but if 20 percent is the best you can see for your type of business (this rate of growth is acceptable in food distribution, menswear, paper products, and bookselling), don't try to fudge the missing growth rate. You probably won't fool a smart investor, and if you do there will be trouble down the road when you don't produce the big returns. Make sure your business plan expresses honestly, exactly, and fully what you have in mind. There is nothing wrong with modifying a plan after receiving the advice of others, including savvy investors who have a great deal to offer business start-ups. Just be sure that the tail of money doesn't wag the dog of inspiration.

An analogy with nonprofit organizations is instructive. As the hopeful grantees read over the "areas of interest" to which well-endowed foundations prefer to give their money, the tendency is to distort existing programs, or even create new ones, in order to match the "needs" of the funding institution. Everyone loses in these situations. The same is true in business.

You must be able to trust yourself and that is why many successful businesses start small, almost stubbornly so: the owners would not compromise and therefore had to fund their start-up with the most meager of resources. On the other hand, many people who have compromised and taken venture capital have found themselves in the private hell of a divided company, with conflicting interests among the owners.

THE PLAN IS NOT THE BUSINESS

A well-developed business plan must be true to your own vision and purpose in order to be a useful tool. It can be a kind of DNA of the enterprise, a powerful template that allows you and your associates to organize what you encounter along the way. The amount of information from the business environment and the marketplace that an individual and company take in over a span of a year is staggering, and this information will have a decided effect on how you run your business. Thus, your business plan will probably be invalid within six months to a year, and you should update it. If you don't, or if the plan is not invalid, you're in trouble because your business isn't growing and changing, and you're not learning. So the specifics of your plan should and will change, but that activity will always be guided by the heart and soul of the plan, your intent, which is steady.

Matthew Reich of Old New York Brewing took about a year to prepare his original 125-page plan, which he has now revised and updated several times. He is a business-man who would find it "impossible" to operate without a plan.

Nevertheless, you must beware of mistaking the plan for the company. You will fare badly if you do. Semanticist Alfred Korzybski's comment that the map is not the territory echoes here: the plan is not the business. But once a territory is mapped, it is never the same for the map-maker, and once a business is well planned, it has already grown in an important way.

PLAN TO LEARN

There is a biology experiment that goes like this:

Frog #1 is placed into a container of water at room temperature. The frog swims.

Frog #2 is placed into a container of extremely hot water. Sensing an inhospitable environment, it immediately jumps out before it is scalded.

Frog #3 is placed in a container of temperate water sitting on a gas burner turned to a low setting. Frog #3 will loll around in the water, swimming. As the water slowly heats up, its senses will dull, and its ability to react will decline. When the animal finally realizes that its environment has changed for the worse and that it will boil to death, it will lack the physical resources to escape unless it is rescued by the compassionate biology student.

Sooner or later, businesses end up like frog #3. Businesses lull themselves into failure, and this often reflects their inability to learn what the immediate business environment is saying. Enterprises fail more often because of the sum total of seemingly inconsequential events acting upon them than because of a sudden disaster or discontinuity.

Once you have learned to plan, you have to plan to learn. When you talk about how to grow a business, you are talking about how to learn. If a business sets itself up as a "knowing" organization, confident of its models and sure of its needs and goals, its perception may be right. But will it be able to learn and change? Only an organization that does not *presume to know* will be able to detect and use fresh new information from its environment. Planning must be firmly based on inquiry. Questions keep a business alive.

The purchases of the first foreign cars in the late fifties were seen by Detroit car makers as a quirky expression of individualism by college students on sophisticated campuses. By the time the American auto industry stopped discounting the superior design, manufacture, and appeal of foreign-made cars, we were in the 1970s, and Detroit had lost its leadership—and some 4 million jobs, directly and indirectly.

The American auto industry has come within a few degrees of the fate of frog #3.

PLAN TO FAIL

I realize this is the opposite of the "dare to be great" school of prosperity. But think about it for a moment. For success to be achieved, many things have to go right. In fact, so many things have to go right that the task of starting a new business might be judged impossible when thoroughly examined, and so many things will go wrong that you will decide that success is something that happens despite your efforts.

If your business plan is based on everything going right, you will be in real difficulty early. You have to look at failure directly, at everything that might go wrong. This examination should go far beyond the conventional break-even analysis that postulates how many units you have to sell to make a profit, how much profit would be created by each subsequent sale, and how price and cost changes would affect profit.

If you conceive and create a business where everything has to go right, one error, one mishap, can ruin a lot of good work. If you conceive a business where twenty serious mistakes could occur, and then you create safeguards to deal with some or most of these possibilities, you are creating a survivor. In the beginning, survival is more important than success. Survival is staying on the field, playing the game, learning the rules, and beginning to grow.

BUSINESS IS THE ART OF
THE INCREMENTAL

The proper way to grow is by releasing growth. The worst way is to push growth. We traditionally look at business growth as centrifugal: reaching out, adding more products, opening more stores, hiring more people. Certainly business must grow, but healthy growth is only that which can be monitored and meted out on your own terms.

In 1986, Yvon Chouinard decided to call a halt, or at least a slowdown, to Patagonia's exponential annual growth rate, which had led to sales of over $40 million annually. He didn't like the fact that he could not remember the names of all three hundred employees. He didn't like the fact that, while he and his wife Malinda were trying to slow things down and regroup, everyone else was urging that the company grow as fast as humanly possible. He was thrilled but concerned when a small Patagonia ad in *The New Yorker* drew the biggest response of any ad of that size ever in the magazine. Chouinard could sense that the natural rate of growth for his company was being pushed aside. He also understood that his company did not need to go to extraordinary lengths to grow and prosper. So in his state-of-the-company speech, delivered in January 1987, Chouinard said that he and Malinda had agreed to go with "whatever *natural* growth rate our companies can comfortably live with, provided that it is consistent with our personal business goals."

Chouinard's personal business goals are:

1. Make money
2. Give money away
3. Be creative
4. Pride
5. No hassles
6. Pfun

Every business has a natural rate of growth. If that rate is not reached, a business can shrivel. If it is surpassed, the business struggles to keep pace. One of the most important functions of the founder/manager of any business is sensing what that "inherent" growth rate should be, and adhering to it. The founder's job is not to lead the "troops" to new heights. Rather, it is to draw out and moderate the changes that will be required of everyone as the business grows.

Japanese accountants have a saying that "over is the beginning of under." The most perilous period in a company's development is when it starts to succeed wildly, enjoys high earnings, and shows rapid sales growth. These three elements can breed mistakes that are masked by outward prosperity. When a recession or other external factor causes sales and profits to decrease, latent errors in judgment and execution are revealed. The time to be expansive is at the bottom of a recession. The time to be conservative and highly cost conscious is when profits and sales are soaring.

We do great damage to our businesses, large and small, when we judge them almost exclusively by their rate of growth. We have the "Inc. 100," the fastest growing public companies in America. But what turmoil lies beneath all of that exponential expansion? Recall the story of the ill-fated NO-KLOG king, the plumber who successfully franchised: I imagine that same scenario is being played out in some of those "Inc. 100" companies.

Do we even have a concept that a slower growing company may be more successful than a fast-growing company? Can we even conceive that speed does not equate with quality, steadfastness, maturity, or even ultimate growth and size? Nothing in nature tells us that rapid growth is good, and certainly nothing in human biology. In our own bodies, the most rapid growth of all is cancer. Are commercial systems so sacrosanct that they are exempt from the logic of morphology as we now see it in all systems?

Ideally, every business student should study biology, the science of life and therefore change. At the heart of the business enterprise is the implementation of true and lasting change, creating the real out of the potential. We are just beginning to understand business as an agent of beneficial change. We need to find out more soon.

We have seen how easily and often our commerce can go wrong, and we tend to overlook where it has gone right and where it may lead us in the future. Fred Smith's Federal Express introduced a valuable new service into our culture, and the company has maintained its edge in the business by operating with enlightenment from top to bottom. The best laboratory for understanding growth—social growth and the growth of individuals—is your own business.

Because I'm in the garden and horticultural business, I am constantly reminded that plants that grow too fast are not really healthy, and that plants growing too slowly are not thriving, either. Temperature, light, humidity, minerals in the soil, and dozens of other variables are critical for proper growth of a plant. For me, business is discovering the commercial and social analogs of heat, light, and moisture.

This is the same understanding that creates a healthy, growing business. You will not wrest success out of an unwilling marketplace. The image of the entrepreneur as a conquering hero is bogus. While the stereotypical qualities of ambition and courage are certainly needed for a start-up enterprise, the opposite qualities are also required. You must be able to sit patiently and listen and observe. You cannot cheat a plant of its nutrients, or force-feed it, without repercussions. Business transactions also require a fair exchange between owner and customer.

It is true that in certain areas, such as computer technology, you have to move quickly or get trampled in the competitive rush. In most businesses that you are likely to start up, however—those not requiring large amounts of capital and technology—you have just enough time to do it and do it right. No more and no less. If you try to speed it up, you won't get it right and will have to do it over.

Do you want to be a mushroom or an oak tree? Spores beat out acorns every time in growth rates, but never in longevity or durability.

Choose as a model for your business a child, a pet, an oak

tree, or some organization you admire. Find one you feel comfortable emulating. Fashion your business in equally healthy ways.

PLAN TO STAY

Plan to be around for a hundred years. Or longer. We all say that a company must continuously strive to give the best service possible. I agree, but that is kind of an abstract idea (which I make more concrete in Chapter 10). If you are planning to be here ten, thirty, seventy years from now, you have to conduct your business as if the world around you will remember everything you have done to date. It will. Even though your business might be involved with a product or technology that is very new, the farther you look ahead in the planning process, the easier it is to realize that the product itself is not the business you are in. Your business is creating satisfaction for the customer, and the means to do that is your new product or service. Technologies, products, and fashions change, but with long-term goals you still have a business.

When Smith & Hawken started, we set out to create a company that would "peak" in the next century. We may or may not be around to witness it, and we may fail, but while we are here we have given ourselves plenty of time. That does not mean we work less hard, but the work has an agenda and timescape that makes us feel relatively unharried and unhassled. While a century may be too long, whenever you plan a new business or a new branch of a business, extend its time frame out far beyond the conventional five-year financial projections and see what it looks like. Then look again. To paraphrase Dorothy Sayers, a business shouldn't be something you do to live, but something you live to do.

PLAN TO SUCCEED

Every business plan paints a rosy future, but few people going into business closely examine the possibility and the results of this hoped-for triumph. If and when it happens, they are unprepared and, often enough, their great success turns into a personal nightmare. We don't have to return to the tale of King Midas to draw vivid examples. Closer to home than myths and legends are the Ivan Boesky and Dennis Levine "success" stories we have all witnessed. Yet the simple message keeps eluding many of us: *how* we go about our business is *what* we attain.

Make money, by all means, but you must have a richer and broader goal than that in mind. Hewlett-Packard states that its first goal is to make money. It wants to do that because its second goal is to grow as a company, and it wants to grow because its third goal is to provide an environment in which more people can thrive. This scenario is explicitly understood at Hewlett-Packard. It's one reason why HP is one of the best corporations in America.

Patagonia has the making of money as its first goal, too. Its second goal is to give a good deal of that money away to nonprofit groups.

Ben & Jerry's ice cream business tithes 7½ percent of its pretax profits to the Ben & Jerry's Foundation, which then distributes it to not-for-profit organizations and charities. That's the highest figure for corporate donations I have heard of. Some of the underwriters of Ben & Jerry's stock issue were concerned about that figure, and wanted to settle on a less specific target contribution. Ben and Jerry believed that the investors they wanted would approve of the generous tithing. The founders must have been right because they never had a problem selling their stock.

Many entrepreneurs say that they intend to do all sorts of wonderful things after their business is successful, but don't when success happens.

I once took over a polymer adhesives business with zero sales, a zero bank balance, and an understandably demoralized staff. It was a poorly run outfit. After a year we made a profit. Two years later I sold it for a handsome sum. Within the corporate charter was a provision that the company would give away 10 percent of all profits. As instructed by the charter provision, I announced at the final board meeting that we the shareholders would now give away that promised 10 percent of the profits of the sale. I was voted down. The shareholders said they needed the money for other purposes. Perhaps, but I believe the shareholders had never honestly prepared themselves for the possibility of success. The 10 percent tithe had been easy to say in the beginning—an unexamined promise. The moral is this: if you plan to succeed, do so from the beginning. There may not be time later.

WRITING THE PLAN

The main problem with even a well-written business plan is easily overlooked. It is written to conform to *outside* expectations, like a résumé. Ever since résumé services came into being, almost every résumé reads the same. They all have right margins justified. Simple job titles have been replaced with expansive euphemisms: salesmen have become field service representatives and janitors are now local area maintenance coordinators. Similarly, people are getting good advice on writing business plans, but the plans are starting to read alarmingly alike. I suggest a different approach.

If you are like me, you choke up at the thought that your business plan will be read by a stranger who will judge you by what is in it. Therefore, forget about the venture capitalist or banker who will read the plan. Imagine instead a friend whose opinion and intelligence you admire, but who knows nothing about your current venture. Write to him or her. Start the plan with Dear Jane and go from there. While you should follow the standard format for a business plan (see below), the first draft can just be a long letter to this understanding person. You will be candid and honest. You will tell your friend what your aspirations and fears are. You will not try to "sell" him or her on your project by employing hyperbole or exaggerated prose. That clear and unadorned language is exactly what a reader of a business plan wants. You may be writing your first or second business plan, but chances are that the people you show it to have read hundreds, sometimes even thousands. They can spot a phony one in the first paragraph. So be yourself, tell the truth, do not be afraid of revealing shortcomings, and when you don't know something, admit it. Keep in mind that *The Wall Street Journal* is written and edited for the comprehension level of a junior high school student. It's a good model.

EXECUTIVE SUMMARY

A business plan usually starts with a summary. I dislike them. If you are passing around your plan to people who are so busy that they need summaries in order to decide whether or not they want to continue, you may be giving it to the wrong people. A summary is also the one item in a business plan that tends to read like all others, so it is tough to make fresh. I think it's optional, and I prefer to start with the purpose of the business, which encapsulates the business but does not reduce it to overly pithy sentences. But most experts disagree with me.

THE NATURE OF THE BUSINESS

This is where you talk about the kind of business you want to create. Remember, this is a description of the whole operation of the business, not merely the product or service. You should explain where the business fits into the larger commercial scheme, how the product or service relates to society, and how the customer perceives or buys the product. This is critical because it is here that you will reveal whether you have market sense. While every reader of a business plan is looking for that unique venture that will excel, business plans that seem so unusual that they are divorced from the everyday vagaries of the market are rather disquieting.

I once received a business plan for a packaged soil nutrient comprised of glacial dust to be distributed through nurseries and garden centers. The rich multimineral mixture showed good results in field tests. The problem with the plan and accompanying literature was its warning that an ice age is impending if we don't start remineralizing the soil with the "proposed" glacial dust. End of business plan.

The description of the nature of your business is not only the opportunity to discuss your vision of the company, but also the time to demonstrate how far out in time you are looking. Short horizons foretell short attention spans. The vast majority of investors are not short-term investors. It is over several or many years that the investor realizes high returns. Ice ages, however, look out too far.

TYPE OF PRODUCT OR SERVICE

Most people go overboard describing their products because it is usually the subject they know the most about. But, once again, a seasoned reader of business plans will read a product description somewhat differently from a first-time reader. First, he will look for something that is shorter and to the point for the simple reason that the better you know your subject, the more succinctly you can express it. Second, if you carry on for page after page describing your widget, the suspicion grows that you are more interested in widgets than business.

I have talked at some length about the need for your business to be an extension of your life and interests, but you don't want your plan to leave the impression that you are going into business *in order to* be more involved with widgets. You may be, but the investor probably isn't. He or she is thinking business and your emphasis might leave the investor wondering how much attention you will pay to the tasks of manufacturing and marketing.

In describing the product, you must have a clear idea of what advantages you are offering the end user. These advantages must not be conceptual or difficult to sell to the customer. In describing advantages, you can show your knowledge of the market by discussing comparative disadvantages of competing products, but dwelling too much on disadvantages does you no good at all. Someone else's stupidity never makes another company smarter.

A MARKETING PLAN

How you are going to get the product to market is as important as what is going to market. Nine out of ten business plans either skip lightly over this point ("we will attend various trade shows, advertise in the pertinent media, and employ sales representatives in outlying territories") or exaggerate their abilities and strengths. Marketing is tough. For a new company or product, a good marketing plan is simple, to the point, and easy to follow. Further, it has contingencies, specific but achievably realistic goals, and does not overstate its objectives. Ideally, the plan does not call for massive expenditures and overhead to begin with, but instead calls for the concerted efforts of a few people, imaginative packaging, presentations, or campaigns, and a highly identifiable audience to address. That's enough—whether you are starting an airline or a daycare center.

COMPETITIVE ANALYSIS

This is where you can shine or tumble. No one wants to hear how terrible another company is. When you first write your plan, you will probably take a dig or two at your competition, but be relentless in editing it out. A compelling competitive analysis is one where respect and in-depth understanding are shown toward competing companies. It is the degree to which you know and understand the competition that speaks well for your plan, not your distaste or feeling of superiority. Ironically, the reader will learn more from this section about the character of the writer than about the character of the competition.

DESCRIPTION OF MANAGEMENT

Once again, suppress the temptation to extol your own or your partners' virtues. If a company, institution, or investor becomes serious after reading your business plan, you want the people they finally meet to match up with the people you describe in the plan. As in all other portions of the business plan, if in doubt, understate. Be modest and forthcoming. Do not pretend your new company has an elaborate management structure. Names and titles mean almost nothing in the beginning, so use them frugally and with restraint. At Smith & Hawken we have one hundred and fifty employees but only the number of titled people required by law—four, president, vice-president, treasurer, and secretary. You do not need a chief financial officer when you are a small company, or a chief operating officer, or an executive vice president. These titles emerge after years of experience in elaborating and differentiating complex organizations. Complexity will come to your business of its own without your imposing it upon the company to begin with. Further, the emphasis in your plan on important titles may indicate that you do not know how to work with a team or group. No one is remotely interested in funding ego trips.

FINANCIAL PROJECTIONS

Projecting financial results five years into the future will be the hardest but most interesting part of creating a business plan. Because a plan is written usually to obtain capital—which is tantamount to receiving permission to exist—it is heavy on projections, assumptions, and market calls. You are asked to assert things you cannot possibly know. You will be faced with the need to project lively growth rates while being true to your own sense of what is possible.

It is rare when a company meets its financial projections. Does this mean you should take them lightly and under-project? Not at all. Financial projections are important because of the thought that goes into them, not because of their putative accuracy in forecasting. You cannot forecast five years into the future without a detailed examination of virtually every single aspect of the business and the economy. Not only are plan and strategy revealed, but so are the myriad details that comprise a successful business. Your understanding and anticipation of these details is what the numbers reveal. It is of vital importance that they be carefully and slowly crafted.

Here again, a seasoned reader of plans will spot innu-merable inconsistencies, omissions, and contradictions. Before presenting financial projections to your true poten-tial investors, be sure to run them by a friend with financial experience who can help you revise them—several times, if necessary. And, finally, be sure that every assumption, every line item, is supported by working notes that you can explain in an oral presentation. This should be no problem. The point of the planning process is to bring you to this degree of knowledge and confidence about your business.

6

The Company
You Keep

MALL BUSINESSES are often structured with the same
foresight with which people buy a house. The young
couple walk in, like the place, go back a second time, read
the termite report, and suddenly they owe more money
than they ever thought possible.

When you "sign the contract" for your new business, you
can't afford to be so cavalier. Buying a house is child's play
compared with entrepreneurship. Even given the fact that
you have a good idea and a good business plan (if you have
decided to be that methodical), you still need the right
foundation on which to build and grow.

Your basic choices are three: sole proprietorship, partnership, or corporation. Sole proprietorships are pretty much just that, but partnerships come in the limited or general flavors, and corporations can be regular or S corporations. Beyond that, the possibilities for structuring debt, equity, and ownership are infinite. All I can do here is suggest the palette available to you as you start out with your business, and my advice, in general, is to do either of two things. Keep it stunningly simple, or make it richly complex and diverse.

SOLE PROPRIETORSHIPS

The vast majority of businesses in Canada and the United States are sole proprietorships because they are the simplest, most direct form of ownership. To start one, you only have to obtain the relevant business license from your local community. If your business will operate under a name other than your own, you will also be required to file a fictitious name statement, usually with the county, and you will have to pay a fee and place an advertisement in the classified ads of a general circulation newspaper so people will know who is really behind the fictitious name. In Canada, you may have to register with the relevant provincial authority.

You will have no legal fees, directors, officers, or stock, and your income taxes are filed on your personal income tax form. Early business losses can be deducted from other income, and all business expenses can be similarly deducted. Unless your business becomes encumbered with debts, you may close it down as quickly as you opened it.

For speed of start-up and autonomy of control, nothing beats the sole proprietorship. But if you intend to grow your business, expand, hire employees, lease or acquire real estate, or take on significant amounts of payables, the sole proprietorship will limit you. The reason is simple: along with the advantage of ownership and control comes the disadvantage of full liability. You are responsible for all the debts. In a later chapter I tell the story of a friend who opened (and closed) a children's clothing store in San Francisco as a sole proprietorship. When it finally foundered and failed, he lost everything—home, vacation house, cars, savings.

You should consider the type and scale of business you are going to start in order to make a correct assessment of the risks. If you intend to sell nosegays to tourists, you have little to worry about. If you're going into the pet grooming business, you may have slightly more concern. What if the shears slip and you accidentally harm a dog? You might be sued. If you are going into the demolition business, you definitely want the safety of incorporation.

Another problem with sole proprietorships is that they have a hard time raising money. Your choices are limited to your own savings and personal borrowing. There is no "official" business for anyone to invest in. Your personal assets will be at stake when you borrow.

The best book on sole proprietorships is *Small-Time Operator*, written and published by Bernard Kamoroff, a C.P.A. whose life exemplifies his book. He owns and operates Bell Spring Publishing in Laytonville, California, whose only function is to publish and promote the book, now in its thirtieth printing.

PARTNERSHIPS

I think partnerships are wonderful. Not easy, but wonderful. The problem is not the partner, but the structure. Legal partnerships are somewhat like marriages and the odds for dissolution are about the same.

As with a sole proprietorship, you are legally inseparable from the business, but in a partnership you are liable not only for your share of liabilities and problems, but for all of them. Each partner is wholly responsible for the actions of the other. If your partner borrows money for the business but spends it on a vacation home, you have to pay the bill. If your partner has marital problems, your business could be forced into liquidation in a settlement of his or her divorce.

I know of a corporation that recently purchased a company after one of the general partners of that company had purchased an airplane for himself and a bed-and-breakfast inn for his girlfriend, all on company funds. The company was for sale because this partner had brought the company to near bankruptcy.

There can be compelling advantages to a partnership. If one partner has ideas and skills and another has the money, that can be a good team. I was once part of such an arrangement. I brought the contacts, he brought the money, and we made a decent living in the food brokerage business until my partner decided he wanted it all and dissolved the partnership while I was out of the country. (Yes, a partnership can be dissolved by either partner without permission of the other.)

There are many variants to partnerships including

limited, nominal, and ostensible partners, as well as secret and silent partners. While you may easily start a sole proprietorship without benefit of a lawyer, I wouldn't recommend setting up a partnership without legal advice. I cannot imagine a business structure that has more S-curves and potholes than a partnership. If it weren't for the tax advantage of passing income and losses directly to the partners, I doubt that partnerships would exist at all.

CORPORATIONS

A corporation is, hands down, the best way to structure most businesses. It is the most elegant institutional construction ever conceived. Corporations are more plastic, motile, adaptable, and mutable than any other form of business organization.

A corporation has that great, stupendous characteristic called "limited liability." The people who own it are not liable, responsible, or accountable for its actions. (Occasionally, directors on boards have been held liable for egregious lapses of judgment, but their liability was not because of their possible ownership, but because they had a managerial or fiduciary responsibility that was abrogated.)

The corporation ranks as one of the most ingenious inventions of mankind, equal to the lever, printing press, and vacuum tube. Taken from the Latin *corpus*, meaning "body," a corporation is just that—a body, but with a twist. It is disembodied and, because of that status, it is also one of the most pernicious creations of the mind of man. Its main virtue for the businessperson—freedom from liability—is also, not surprisingly, its bane. The corporation can do good deeds or commit crimes, save or kill. Before the corporation, the only institutions with this kind of power and independence were the church and the state. When the corporation was introduced, it became the third player in the triumvirate that still rules the world.

Corporations have been around for centuries and have developed a ritualized process of doing business, resolving conflict, growing, changing, developing, and interacting with society as a whole. In other words, a corporation is a scripted and well-defined structural relationship between shareholders, directors, officers, and employees that has yet to be improved upon. As your business grows your corporation can grow, developing and becoming more complex and differentiated with age. Remember that a corporation can be a for-profit, a nonprofit, a cooperative, a family farm, or a go-for-the-throat unprincipled slob in the world of commerce. In all four cases, the corporate structure works beautifully.

A corporation is nurtured and kept functioning by people, but it does not depend on any particular persons. A corporation can be bought, divided, sold, bought back, killed, or put on a shelf. As we have seen recently, corporations can be raided, broken apart, and dismembered in a matter of weeks. They can be publicly owned or they can be so private that their activities are largely unknown, like the Southern Air Transport Co. whose plane was shot down over Nicaragua in 1986.

Because it is not any one individual, a corporation that is properly run and organized represents the interests of the whole rather than any one person or interest. Of course, this is not true when a corporation is owned by one person. But in the much more common case in which the corporation is owned by many parties, it is without doubt the most civilized way in which people can pool their common interests and pursuits while minimizing conflict.

The expense of creating and maintaining a corporation is negligible compared to its benefits. But keep the following problems, questions, nuances, and oddities in mind as you think about your requirements.

HAVE A PARTNER

Even within the corporate structure, in my opinion you will need a partner. You shouldn't even think of going it alone. I say this even though I've been burned by a partner. In general, though, partners make the good times more fun, the hard times more bearable. A partner is someone to talk, debate, noodle, and argue with. Someone to grow with. And you should have this partner from the very beginning because that's the only way to assure absolute parity. A "full" partner brought in a year after start-up is not really a full partner.

A corollary of "have a partner" is "have the right partner." By the time I started Smith & Hawken I knew how important the other people are in a business, and that goes double for the partner. I wanted a person whose integrity was so intact that, regardless of success or failure, he would remain the same person. I didn't care about previous business experience, contacts, personal wealth, or even whether he knew a whit about tools and gardening. I

111

just wanted somebody I could totally trust and that's why I chose Dave Smith. I would make the same choice today. The business might have gone quicker and easier if I had chosen a partner who was more knowledgeable about the business, but our reason for teaming up was simply that we wanted to work together. The best reason of all.

WHO SHOULD OWN
YOUR COMPANY?

You should. After that, the possibilities are endless. A consistent mistake companies make is not including their employees as owners. The error results from the illusion that there is "less" company to go around if the ownership is spread around. If your intent is to grow your company (so we are not talking about a newsstand right now) you are going to need every bit of help, energy, luck, and assistance possible. The only rational way to structure a company is in such a way that you would work well within it. In other words, you should create a company you would want to be the employee of, not merely the boss of. If you don't do that, you have instituted a double standard which will pervade the company and cause trouble. This is a major belief of mine, and it bears repeating.

The theory behind the "double standard" structure includes such assumptions as: you started the company, they didn't, so you deserve everything you can get; you took the risk, you get the reward; if your workers were as smart and as enterprising as you, they would have their own company and wouldn't have to complain or be envious of your position; a living wage is sufficient, why pay more?

This standard is usually enforced in unsubtle ways, including dress, company cars, separate bathroom, deluxe office for you but cubbies for the clerks, and a host of other signals that tell your employees to keep their distance, know their place, respect your position and status. Most companies are organized this way—worldwide. The Japanese come closest to breaking this mold, but much of their camaraderie is superficial and depends on powerful cultural boundaries which cannot be transgressed by any worker without fear of censure.

Most companies are organized without employee ownership and the world of commerce has grown to gargantuan proportions without it. Surely this proves that a system of excluding workers from ownership works well enough. Or has worked well enough in the past. But the world of commerce is changing radically, and I believe for the better, as customers and employees exert pressure for better products and service—better companies. And companies are better if the workers share in the ownership.

Springfield Remanufacturing Center in Missouri instituted an Employee Stock Ownership Plan (ESOP) as an integral part of the buyout from International Harvester. Today, four hundred thousand of the 3 million shares of stock outstanding are vested in the ESOP. Every year a portion of earnings is used to purchase unissued stock for the ownership plan. The plan makes The Great Game of Business at Springfield Remanufacturing even more fun.

Ask someone who works for a company if 100 percent of his or her intelligence, creativity, energy, and abilities is being utilized and nurtured. Most people, most of the time, hold something or even a lot back from their employers. This doesn't mean they are not bone-weary at night; they are, and part of the reason they are is because of this restraint. It's tiring not to put your heart and soul into your work. It's enervating to play office politics, to have to create power bases for yourself, to compete with others for position and salary, to worry about your backside when you are trying to get a job done. It's frustrating to pour yourself into a job or project and watch another person take the credit, and yet another walk off with the profits.

Like canny investors, employees know exactly how much of themselves they will invest in a given work situation before they feel taken for granted or ripped off. For pragmatic reasons of productivity and employee satisfaction, if for no other reason, I advise employee ownership. Nevertheless, it is not a panacea. If it is instituted as a "technique," it has no meaning and can backfire. There is no point in sharing equity if it does not stem from your sense of fairness. If you are not a fair person, don't fake it. Employees resent hypocrisy more than greed.

Fairness is something people feel. You cannot fool workers with fancy titles, by calling people "associates" or holding pep rallies, or by convoluted profit-sharing schemes that vest on the seventieth birthday. So often in business literature the question comes up as to what is the best way to treat your employees. It is a question with no meaning. The question you should always ask is what do you think of your employees. What you think about the people you work with will decide how you treat them, and will determine how you structure your company.

A few years back, there was a company with about $100 million in sales that prided itself on being one of the three "humanistic" corporations in America. That was their description, not mine. I remember it well because we were starting Smith & Hawken and pondering the very questions this chapter addresses when that company—let's call it the Rainbow Sky Company—consulted with me on their new corporate charter. After years of what seemed to be an enlightened corporate policy, management was putting the final touches on a new charter that would be even better. It was an inch thick, one of the most complicated corporate charters I have ever read.

Each "benefit" that an employee received, whether stock ownership or profit sharing, was given or vested in such a complex manner that no employee (or the lawyers, I'll bet) could readily understand or remember it on one reading. There were many provisos and hurdles—for example, stock ownership had to be relinquished on a somewhat punitive basis if a person chose to leave the company. The new charter wasn't fair, generous, or "humanistic." It was simply a new way of being patrimonious.

No rules, charters, precepts, tenets, or corporate hoo-haw will make you or anyone else a better person. Either you are a good company to work for or you are not; you are either good to your employees or you are not; you either share with others or you do not. No amount of puffery can hide the facts. So if you are going to have a profit-sharing program in your company, be sure you want to share. A company that shares profits should also be willing to share responsibility, authority, praise, credit, and a good joke. Money is never a substitute for esteem, pride, and dignity, and profit sharing without a sense of sharing is nothing but piecework.

Equity, whether in the form of incentive-type options, ESOPs, grants, loans, or pooled interests, should have the single purpose of creating a sense of shared condition: we are in this together and will act accordingly. This does not mean that founders relinquish authority, or that management is no longer required on all levels of the organization, or that each staff member is now primarily accountable to self. It does mean that owners recognize that in a successful company each individual creates more worth than his or her wages reflect, and that if some of that value is returned to the managers and staff, everyone benefits: the employees, the shareholders, and the customers.

Compensation consultants will debate whether profit-sharing programs should be formulaic (based on some predetermined relationship between profits, productivity, and/or sales), or whether their administration should be discretionary, based on performance, initiative, and creativity. We have the latter at Smith & Hawken, but many companies do use formulas. Either way is fine as long as it is consistent, fair, and true to all other aspects of the company and your actions.

An alternative to an employee ownership plan that accomplishes the same goal—a sense of shared condition— is Ben & Jerry's compensation formula, a modification of a plan made famous by the Mondragon workers' cooperative in the Basque region of Spain. At Ben & Jerry's, no employee earns less than one-fifth of the highest salary paid, including all perks. If Ben and Jerry as the founders are paid $60,000 apiece, no one earns less than $12,000.

BE DIVISIBLE

This advice applies to partnerships as well as corporations. The main thing wrong with the structure of a partnership is that the patient often dies when it is divided. Even when businesses survive after a partnership dissolves, there may be a rancorous and bitter residue. Before you put your business partnership together on paper, figure out how you are going to take it apart if forced to. Divorces, lawsuits, and changes of heart can tear a business apart. If you are going into business with friends or associates, as a corporation or partnership, you should discuss and agree on how each person will be able either to get out or retain control should the worst-case scenario occur. If such discussions are uncomfortable and too difficult to countenance, you might want to reexamine your association with your partners right then.

DON'T PAY RETAIL

Three types of professionals will gladly structure or help structure your business for you: lawyers, accountants, and general business consultants. Go easy on them. You must do things properly but, unless you have deep pockets, you will have to get a business off the ground with minimal expense and encumbrance from the professions.

In the movie *Goodbye Columbus*, Richard Benjamin and Ali Macgraw have their first fight and she tearfully sobs that the biggest sin in her family is to raise one's voice. Benjamin looks at her incredulously and says that the

biggest sin in his family is to buy something retail. Paying
for legal and accounting services at retail prices in the
beginning is a sin. Professionals and consultants who take
advantage of new business start-ups should be admonished.
But since your lawyer is not likely to cut the hourly fee, all
you can do is substitute your preparation, learning, and
decision-making ability for his or her time. Lawyers work
for you. You never want one giving unsolicited advice on
your time. Anytime one does, ask him to turn off his meter.
Above all, do not be intimidated.

The problem with lawyers is not that they don't know
enough. They know too much. They know everything that
might go wrong. They know thousands of ways to structure
a business. They know thousands of ways that you and they
can get sued, too. Whenever they are asked to get involved
with a new business start-up that involves raising capital,
the larger firms will put a healthy amount of legal time on
your bill to pay for their malpractice insurance, and to
make sure neither of you is potentially liable.

When you are structuring your business, accountants can
be helpful, too. Most of the Big Eight accounting firms
have "sprout groups" whose purpose is to nurture small
business start-ups into good-paying, medium-sized clients.
Avoid them. So far, most are too new and too removed
from the actual day-to-day needs of a small business to be
of any help. The Big Eight firms will use these sprout
groups as training ground for their new staff and starting
interns. Thus their lower rates and dewy cheeks. They
should pay you because in most instances they are using
your business to season their staff. We have tried sprout
groups at Smith & Hawken, and found that we spent at

least as much time training the accountants as they spent auditing and reviewing our books. A crusty old C.P.A. will be more helpful than a gaggle of recent graduates.

The good news in all this is that the juiciest source of information on how to structure your business is not the professional anyway. Your best bet is other businesspeople. Today, in communities across the country, fledgling entrepreneurs and start-ups meet and caucus under various guises. These are the people you should consult with. Their advice is free, and their mistakes are as interesting as their successes.

THE LIVING STRUCTURE

Ideally the structure you establish for your business will be a living one. But in reality it may be one that is difficult to change or root out. So, whatever form your business takes, it should accurately reflect your own needs. You are creating an organizational structure simply by being who you are.

The organization that you are going to be most comfortable running is one where you would work best if you were an employee. If this is a tight, hierarchical organization, with management by directive and a crisp, no-nonsense chain of command, you shouldn't mess around with amorphous forms of organization. Engineering-oriented companies thrive under tighter forms of leadership, but even here there are exceptions, such as the design group of the Macintosh at Apple Computer.

I have worked for myself almost my entire adult life and,

when I was an employee, I did not like it. Naturally, my company does not have a tight organizational chart, because I would feel suffocated by it, as "boss" or employee. People at Smith & Hawken are given a lot of responsibility and a minimum of supervision. The structure is "flat" as opposed to pyramid-like. Maybe it's an odd duck. It certainly doesn't conform to the usual structures, but your company probably won't either. Don't worry about it. But do remember George Bernard Shaw's admonition: "Take care to get born well."

7

Money

H OW CAN we ever learn to handle money when most of us have never had enough of it, and a precious few have had way too much? I was part of the middle class and stayed there until my family blew apart at the seams when I was eight. My parents divorced, and the three kids were split off to different relatives. We never did reassemble as a family. I ended up practically on welfare and remember a Christmas dinner of corn flakes and warm powdered milk. There were no presents or tree. I have told this story to fewer than six people in my life because it evokes a sympathy which is now beside the point. I relate it here because it illustrates the problem most of us have had: at some point in our lives, we have suffered indignities caused by lack of money. If we have not experienced this embarrassment directly, we have seen its effect on others. If we couple these experiences with the covetousness that is engendered by television, movies, and the magazines, and add to that the experience of the sixties, when much of a generation developed a contempt for money, the net result is a society that is ill prepared to understand and work with money. There's just too much extra baggage associated with it. We can't disentangle the relationship among money, people, and business.

Money, then, is the last taboo, for people and their businesses. People are usually willing to discuss their religious and sexual proclivities, but ask a friend or relative what his net worth is and he will probably be offended. If I should include in this book a detailed picture of my income, assets, and worth, it would be unseemly and the reader would be uncomfortable. Not so if I should announce that I am gay, straight, or celibate.

Ask the owner of a privately held business how much money he makes and you will not only encounter the taboo, you may also find someone who defines his worth in terms of money: the proverbial bottom line.

It sounds fatuous for me to say that money is not a problem for businesspeople, but that's what I want to say. Research into small business failure has shown that most fail because of a lack of working capital. But that's like saying that the cause of most divorces is conflict. The question is, What causes the lack of working capital? Earlier, I said that too much money, not too little, was a bigger problem for most small businesses. In a business, money does not create anything at all, much less ideas and initiative. Money goes where those qualities already are. Money follows, it does not lead. As a businessperson, you foster money with thought, strategy, demeanor, and deed.

I will discuss money in this chapter without the usual textbook pondering of return on equity, acid tests, inventory returns, or debt-to-equity ratios. These and other financial measurements are critical to business success, but they are so widely discussed and referenced that there's little I could add to the pool of technical knowledge. What is seldom addressed is our attitude toward money, and this attitude precedes and affects the start-up and growth of a business, and everyone involved. The fact that much of the handling of money is precise, almost mechanistic, hides the churning unease and discomfort almost all of us have with it.

Let your relationship with money determine the amount of money you use to start your business. I started Erewhon, my first business, with $500, and Smith & Hawken with $100,000. In 1967 I would have felt uncomfortable with more than $500, but a little over a decade later I would have been uncomfortable with less than the $100,000. The difference was not a result of the different nature of the two businesses, but the nature of my attitude toward money. When I started out at Erewhon, I was unsure of myself and of money in general, and I had a lot to learn.

You should start a business with just as much capital as makes you feel comfortable, and you should obtain it from the sources you are most comfortable with.

At Smith & Hawken, we started small despite our access to larger amounts of money. My business experience could have attracted that capital, and did so as we grew, but that experience had also taught me to start small. We placed an order for one container of tools costing $25,000, due to arrive from Bulldog Tool Company in England around Thanksgiving Day, 1979. In the meantime we placed one-inch ads in *Organic Gardening, The New Yorker, New Farm,* and a couple of other magazines. Those one-inch ads (the smallest sold) are the kind used to sell elevator heels, EEEEE shoes, necktie narrowing services, and Authentic Missouri Sorghum Cookbooks.

We showed a picture of one of our forks with the header "ENGLISH GARDENING TOOLS. Send for free catalog . . ." Our address was 68 Homer, Palo Alto, CA. We ran the ad for four months and received 497 requests for the catalog. But we didn't have a catalog. We had to create the business first.

Dave Smith and I found space in the vestigial industrial section of Palo Alto. We were wedged between the Southern Pacific tracks, a lumberyard, a tool rental company (our landlord), and a pipefitter's storage yard. We had two throwaway desks, two phones, a piece of used carpet between us, and one thousand square feet of empty warehouse. We had no windows, no heat, and no privacy. Because of fire laws, our landlord and her employees could walk through anytime day or night, and did. Sometimes we had to call customers back because our neighbors were testing chainsaws or compressors in the adjacent repair room and we couldn't hear a thing. Other customers or, a little later, suppliers, couldn't find us. Even local residents didn't know where 68 Homer was. (After a year we were more confident of our prospects, so we put up a sign made by a hitchhiking art student I had given a ride. It cost, appropriately, $68. Things were looking up.)

When the back door of the container swung open and revealed our first load of tools, Dave and I were excited, to say the least, even though we had nothing but a borrowed cart from the tool rental company to unload it with. Since virtually all of the English tools were unknown in the U.S. market, I had ordered a wide variety. If we were going to be different, why not go all the way? As we unloaded, I had second thoughts. As tool after unusual tool was revealed, our venture began to seem less like a business than an anthropological dig. Not content to order a straightforward garden fork, I had also ordered a thirteen-pound Sri Lankan solid metal Tea Plantation Fork with thirteen-inch tines as thick as a baby's ankle (later dubbed and sold as the Monster Fork). Behind that were my long-handled Irish Dunse Slashers, used for making hedgerows in County Cork, five-pronged Scottish Manure Forks, the Royal British Mail Rabbitting Spade (I still don't know what that name refers to), and the fourteen-pronged, ball-capped "Swede" fork. (I later found out that this last one wasn't used by Swedes, but that it was used to till rutabagas. When I subsequently asked a Scotsman why his country-men called rutabagas "swedes," his eyes twinkled. "I had heard it said that rutabagas are short, blond, and fat, but knowing me countrymen, and being part Scots yourself, you wouldn't think they'd be so keen as to notice the similarity, would you?")

When the tools—2,500 implements—were all stowed in the warehouse, Ray, the foreman of the tool rental shop who had recently arrived in California from Oklahoma, walked back and forth among them. I sensed he was trying to think of something he could say that would come out as a compliment. He was struggling. I felt like an immigrant who had refused to assimilate. Ray finally said, "Well, they look strong enough," and he never said another word about them in the three years we shared the warehouse.

Later that day, a couple from the Philo Pottery near Boonville, California, drove up, picked out $126 worth of tools, and wrote a check. When we asked them how they knew about the company, the tools, or the first delivery that morning, they replied that they had heard about it from friends. Unknowingly, they had started Smith & Hawken.

There is no reason in the world to start a business that makes you overly anxious about money—whether you'll lose it, how to pay it back, and so on. Embarking on your first business venture, you should start slowly and steadily, preferably using your own money. That way you don't have to worry about interest payments, payback schedules, or loss of face. And if you borrow from yourself, you will have the right attitude about money right away, which is that it's hard to come by and hard to keep. It's easy to remember this with your own money, but you can lose perspective when spending borrowed money or invested capital.

"How long should a man's legs be? Long enough to reach the ground," Lincoln said. How much money does a business need? You need enough money to get to market. A bootstrap operation places you in the heart of the market sooner than any other business structure. Without capital, you will have to sell something immediately in order to establish a cash flow. To attract this quick acceptance, your product or service will have to be good and practical—like a pint of Ben & Jerry's Heath Bar Crunch ice cream. Bootstrapping gives you a tremendous advantage, revealing the strengths and weaknesses in your business better than a thousand preliminary studies and surveys could do. Just as hunger will make you alert, so lack of capital will make you keenly aware of the business environment.

Bootstrap businesses will act like a malnourished child. These businesses cry for money, and you, the owner, won't be able to get the money problem out of your head as you scrape and scrounge to get your business off the ground. But after the business is established you will understand that it wasn't new sources of money that held the key, after all, but the pluck and initiative you had to develop along the way. With low overhead, frugal means, and fragile budgets, you can't buy your way out of problems. You have to learn your way out. The creativity and tenacity you have to develop will make it hard for you to be put out of business. Likewise, if you are the first business in your niche in your town, you will have an advantage that money and power cannot overcome: the first sperm penetrating the egg seals it to all the others.

Here is my recipe for successfully financing a bootstrap operation, one that has worked for me because it is true to my own needs and my concerns with security, loss of capital, and business growth.

START SMALL

The virtue and strength of the bootstrap business are in its smallness, so don't ruin this with large infusions of easy money. Learn on your own nickel. I don't mean taking out a second or third mortgage on your house, or cashing the children's savings bonds. I mean a business that can be funded from your own savings. Your mistakes will not embarrass you, because you paid for them. It's okay to start part time, to moonlight, to hold two jobs, to hedge and to play it safe. Alice Medrich of Cocolat was still in business school when she first began selling her chocolate truffles wholesale. If you start too large, you are faced with lenders and investors before you even have a chance to get involved with the market.

Forget about making money at first. Look at the first few months or year as tuition. If you do make money early, fine, but when you start a business, consider it a screaming success if it does not lose money. You are lending money to your own business in order to learn whether it is worth expanding, and whether it is something you want to devote many years to, whether it is something the market is interested in. You want to learn the essential facts about the business without getting mired in it should your initial guess be proved wrong. Overnight successes make fabulous reading (Compaq Computer Corp. had $111 million in first-year sales with a business plan drawn up on a napkin). They make us plodders wonder whether there wasn't something we could have done to be so brilliant. Probably not, if your new business isn't a major advance in computers. Besides, the vast majority of success stories are written by the plodders.

During the first year we plodders should be talking with relatives, friends, bankers, and any other conceivable source of future funding. Tell everyone what the idea is, how you started up, what the goals are. Describe ups and downs, what you have learned, how you can improve. Be forthright and candid. If you are offered cash, loans, or advice, accept only the latter. Demur on the money but ask people whether, should the need arise, you could call on them at a later time.

Always try to avoid having to pop the question of money. Draw people out so that they are offering it or, if not offering it, at least thinking about it. This is not a ploy. It's easier to ask someone for a date if he or she has said earlier, "Let's go out sometime."

If the relative or friend brings up the subject of money first, a very different relationship is established. But he or she cannot and will not do this unless you openly discuss your business. And by being forthcoming, you are providing the means for people to assess your ability to do what you say you will. If you say that next month you will do something, and then do it, people notice. Just as banks lend money when you don't need it, we want to loan or invest money in a business that is succeeding and may not need us. The sense that someone is on track, on schedule, and on purpose is immensely attractive to people and capital.

FINANCE BEFORE YOU NEED
THE MONEY

As your business grows, you will soon need cash, even if your operation is a frugal bootstrap. For three reasons, you should always obtain that money before you need it.

First, this will give you plenty of time to discuss your

financing needs with a wide variety of sources. This way you can obtain the best terms and deal with people or institutions you're most comfortable with, with a feeling on both sides that the decision was mutual.

Second, desperation repels. It always provokes the question, usually unspoken, Why are you in such bad shape if you're such a great businessperson? Good question for which there is rarely a ready answer.

Third, desperation means the lender or investor dictates the terms—usually take it or leave it.

And remember at all times that the litmus test we are using for money is the sense of ease and comfort it gives you. Money should not cause a mental rash. Grow your business with that in mind and you will have an inbuilt arbiter of healthy development. It is not a question of whether your business should grow at 10 percent or 150 percent. Do not compare yourself with others. Ignore the journalistic sirens of quick success. The question is what growth rate is comfortable for you. You are what this business is all about.

BORROWING FROM FRIENDS

Friends are the first source of money for most small businesses. But this is a touchy subject, because I have never heard of an unrepaid personal loan that did not cause bad feelings. Therefore, don't even think of borrowing money to start your business unless you are willing to pay it back—personally. Your ability to secure greater amounts of capital from increasingly diverse sources de-

pends on one all-important criterion—character. Your
honor and trustworthiness are all you have, and how you
treat and respect other people's money will be one of the
primary factors by which you are judged.

Another sensitive issue when borrowing from friends or
relatives is control of the business. Misunderstandings form
easily. Many people who lend money "privately" think that
this gives them some authority or at least say-so in the
business. Be sure to borrow from someone who understands that you want to be free to operate the business
yourself.

Matthew Reich, founder of Old New York Brewery Co.,
raised most of a quarter of a million dollars from friends and
acquaintances. A few of those investors aren't talking to
him anymore. They wanted to see an immediate cash flow,
or they felt that Reich was diluting their ownership and
giving away control when he went into the equity market to
raise $4 million. The original investor's percentage share in
the company dropped if he or she didn't put up more
money.

The issue here is not one of right or wrong. The issue is
the difficulty of dealing with friends when a lot of questions
may not get asked and therefore answered. It is a pervasive
problem in small businesses. Sometimes enemies understand each other better than friends do.

Lenders may inquire about ownership or partnership or
an equity position. If you do issue stock or disperse
ownership, make it clear that passive ownership is different
from operating the company. When I started one of my
companies, a friend who had done me a very great favor
asked if I wouldn't sell some stock to her son, who had

inherited a lot of money and needed to invest some of it. I did so, as a favor. Within weeks, the son was pestering the company. Within months, he tried to take it over.

I hope I don't sound too negative about money. Granted, if you have little or no business experience, your sources of capital are extremely limited. But rather than fight it, accede to the situation and make it work for you. Like a stairway, the access to capital is gained in increments of successful loans and paybacks. Don't try to take six steps at a time.

I knew an executive who worked for twelve years at a successful company, and had achieved a vice presidency. Still young, he quit his job, took his stock profits, mortgaged his house, borrowed from friends, and started a new business in equipment rental. He began with two locations and had to grow fast in order to service the interest on the heavy borrowing. He borrowed still more money to keep the business afloat, but to no avail. The business went under.

He rejoined the corporate world, once more making a high salary, but his debts from the failed business meant he couldn't live on the salary. He was in the hole $1,000 a month, and he was under intense personal strain at home. I tell this story because we rarely hear these tales. We usually read about the person who bet the farm and came up roses. We are emboldened and charged up by such stories. And deluded. The person who started the equipment rental business had worked well for twelve years but he had never owned or operated his own business. Owning a business and working for one are as different as chalk and cheese.

If he had understood this when he started out on his own, he would have settled for one store, maybe a partnership, maybe a franchise—anything before he committed so much of his own and other people's funds. He borrowed money he could not, and still cannot, repay. He is a conscientious person, and this failure bothers him greatly. It's a burden that affects the whole fabric of his life.

If you get nothing else from this book, at least understand that starting a business should not mean creating a living hell for yourself. The quickest way to create this hell is to borrow too much money.

The alternative to bootstrapping in starting a new business is what I call the under/over approach. It begins with all those expenditures that would actually harm the bootstrap: marketing studies, planning, analysis, and detailed anticipation of capital requirements. This approach is "under/over" because the business will go through a start-up period of perhaps a year, or several, in which it will be "under" breakeven, losing money. It will eat capital in its attempt to grow to a size sufficient to reverse the cost disadvantages. Later profits will theoretically make up for early losses.

Under/over is enhanced by passion, dedication, and the tremendous energy and hard work required of bootstrappers, but in addition it requires prior business experience, training, and commercial skills that will, or should, enable the founders to see through the smokescreen that may be thrown up by all the marketing studies and spreadsheet calculations. Last but not least, under/over needs ready access to capital.

I don't know of any study comparing the success rate of the two different approaches to new business, but I don't need the figures to know that the bootstrap works better for most small businesses. I recommend it for your probable business, sight unseen.

However, if you attempt to grow a large business in a short time, you are less likely to reach your goals using bootstrap methods, and you will more likely need the traditional business methods. And some businesses, certainly high-tech ventures and even Matthew Reich's New York brewery, simply require more money going in than, say, Ben and Jerry's first ice cream parlor.

The main problem with the ambitious under/over method is this: unless you and your partners (and you probably will have partners) are well versed, well connected, or have an extraordinary product or idea, you will find it a difficult way to raise capital. It's almost impossible to go cold into the world and raise money from strangers. Matthew Reich had been a loan officer at a bank but that didn't do him any good. He knew no bank was going to lend him money, and the odds were not good for venture capital. In fact, the odds of a business attracting significant venture capital are one in ten thousand.

A friend who worked in the beverage industry for many years quit his job and has now spent seven years trying to start a true cold-filtered Bavarian batch brewery in California. At this writing, he is trying to raise $5 million. Every year the amount he needs goes up, not down, and his chances of success continue to recede. He started his brewery idea at the same time Reich started his company with a more modest $250,000. Today New Amsterdam has sales of $4 million. Is this a tortoise-and-hare fable? Yes, I think so.

THE PERU SYNDROME

Because the great money-center banks of the United States have made a decade's worth of ridiculous loans to Third World countries, real estate partnerships, energy companies, and overextended farmers, they make sure that every small business jumps through all the hoops that the bad loans should have encountered, but didn't. Despite the fact that the banks have far lower losses from small businesses than from large, it is exponentially more difficult for a small business to get a loan. I call this the Peru syndrome, in honor of the first of the Third World countries to suspend interest payments on its multibillion-dollar loans. We are seeing the banking world's version of closing the barn doors. (An ad for the University National Bank shows a scowling military dictator below the headline, DON'T CRY FOR ME, ARGENTINA. The bank doesn't have a part of any of those multibillion-dollar loans.)

A bank is the most conservative of all possible sources of capital for a small business. You could argue that it is in the business of losing only large amounts of capital, never small. So your bank loan will be secured at least two ways, by collateral and by your personal assets.

This telling example: Smith & Hawken, with sales (at the time) of several million, with no debt and a high net worth, could not get a real estate loan from the Bank of America to buy the building we occupied. Right after that, the bank started a series of TV and newspaper ads claiming that they were the friend of the small businessperson.

Ironically, that was once true. A. P. Giannini started the bank in 1904 because he thought the small customer was being unfairly treated by other banks. His bankers would lend out money without collateral, relying on the applicant's character and their own gut feelings. Soon the bank was known as "The Little Fellow's Bank." The little fellows that owe the most money to Bank of America eighty years later are Brazil and Mexico.

The flip side of borrowing from a bank is doing business with it. Again, because banking has become highly centralized in ownership, small businesses tend to get lost in the cracks. As a retailer, Smith & Hawken puts VISA and MasterCard slips through a bank, a "deposit" that is very profitable because the bank retains a percentage of the transaction. Our first bank, Bank of America, once double-charged our customers by mistake. This made us look fairly bad in our customers' eyes. We asked the bank to send them a letter, which they did somewhat reluctantly. The letter was so ambiguously worded that the recipient couldn't be certain whose mistake it was, the bank's or ours. When the bank triple-charged the customers a few months later, we thought it time to find another bank.

I called Wells Fargo, two blocks from our offices, one of hundreds of branches of the seventh largest bank in the United States, and said we wanted to shift our charge card deposits to a new bank. The manager had never heard of Smith & Hawken, one of the largest businesses in our small town. When he heard that we were in the catalog business, he said he didn't think the bank wanted our business because mail order companies were so flaky. But he said he might consider us if we brought in three years of audited financials. Remember that these deposits are a service on which the bank makes good money. But Wells Fargo was busy acquiring Crocker Bank at the time.

Moral: If your town has a truly local bank, you may fare better there because the social bonds that hold a community together allow for greater latitude in dispensing loans and other banking services.

If you do borrow from a bank, prepare a loan application that will knock the bankers' argyles off. Remember that most bank managers and loan officers have never run a business and live in mortal dread that they might have to someday. This is why your business is insufficient collateral. Bankers need help. At best, most bankers will know well only one or maybe two types of businesses. Chances are your business will be a mystery to them. Rather than say candidly that they don't have a clue how the ice cream business works, they'll try to look intelligent and ask questions. You can help things along by presubmitting a thorough application that you have drawn up yourself. When you meet to discuss the loan request, the banker will be more fully informed about your business, will be more comfortable talking about it, and then can more easily champion it before the loan committee.

After your loan is approved, however, don't be surprised if they ask for your firstborn as collateral.

BORROWING FROM THE SBA

One of the strangest institutions known to mankind is the Small Business Administration. If you have free time on your hands and are interested in what I call "commercial anthropology," you should by all means apply to the SBA for a loan. It is an unforgettable experience, but it won't be a cliffhanger. You may wait a year to eighteen months for approval or rejection. This is assuming you have qualified as a small business. Their definitions are interesting. Don't assume that your hardware store with eight employees is a small business. In 1980, such a business in the U.S. was classified as a big business and ruled ineligible—while a manufacturing company with 2,500 employees could apply for a loan.

The SBA is the lender of last resort. Although the rules vary according to the size of the town, you generally have to be turned down by two banks before you are worthy of an SBA loan. Two types of SBA loans are possible: business loans and economic opportunity loans.

Business loans can be granted for purchase of real estate, machinery, equipment, and supplies. They can also be used for general business expansion, inventory, and working capital. Loans of up to $500,000 are theoretically possible, but they're rare. Payback periods vary from a few to ten years, and in some cases twenty years for real estate.

Economic opportunity loans are like business loans except that they are targeted to disadvantaged persons, either of low income or minority status, who have been consistently excluded from the opportunities of starting or owning a business. For these individuals, the Small Business Administration is a good bet.

Different rules apply in Canada where the SBA is part of the Federal Business Development Bank. Whatever it's called, they turned down publisher Jim Lawrence when he was starting up his highly successful magazine, *Harrow-*

smith. Likewise, Ben Cohen and Jerry Greenfield obtained provisional approval for their small SBA loan but then the site they selected for their store was disapproved. They went ahead without the loan.

But the main problem with the SBA is this: by the time they have moved, you will have, too. If you are a small, growing business, it is almost impossible to wait the allotted year or more for an answer. An eighteen-month waiting period for a rapidly growing business is an absurdity. You will either be larger or gone by that time.

BORROW A LOT OR NONE

In the case of banks: if you decide to borrow, you may want to borrow as much as you can. If you are leveraged to the teeth, at least people will think twice about messing with you. (You may also get an ulcer.)

At one point in my food business days, I had amassed and drawn over a million dollars on my line of credit from the bank. Those were ninety-day notes customarily rolled over by the bank. The loans exceeded Erewhon's net worth by a factor of five and, when President Nixon put in wage and price controls in 1971–72, interest rates soared to the then-historic high of 13 percent. Bank examiners audited our loan package and discovered that, with the high interest rates, we no longer "qualified" for the loans: our higher interest payments were too large a percentage of our cash flow. The bank was forced to call the notes.

Disaster—for any business. I began paying down the notes as they came due ($30,000 to $50,000 per week) but

I could no longer pay the bills. Suppliers were angry. Payrolls were kited. The solution to my problem seems obvious in retrospect, but it took an agonizing few weeks of tribulation before I cottoned on.

One Monday morning, I called the vice president of the bank and told him in my best Boston accent to back off or he wouldn't get a cent. An extraordinary thing happened. I, who had always minced into the bank with my hat in my hand, was invited to the executive dining room on the forty-eighth floor of the Prudential Tower. I was treated to original Japanese art, Coquilles St. Jacques, fresh strawberries and asparagus in February, and for dessert a mellifluous flow of sugary words from management.

As soon as I became a problem, I was treated with the kind of attention accorded a good customer. In their eyes, I became a "good" customer once I'd become a bad one. I finally realized what they had known all along: given the nature of my business and my assets, there was not a whole lot they could do to force me to pay off the loan. I suspect some of those bankers were the same ones who proceeded to become the international loan group now handling the Brazil, Mexico, and Peru portfolios.

All this confirms the maxim of Fred Smith, founder of Federal Express: "The worst that can happen if you borrow a lot is that you have a new partner."

That's the worst that can happen *if you're Fred Smith*. But if you don't want to be leveraged up to your eyeballs, this brinksmanship might create that living hell I mentioned before. You decide.

* * *

Before the advent of venture capitalists and stock exchanges, businesses were quite capable of raising capital by selling equity in their corporations directly to individuals. In recent years, due to red tape, fear of litigation, and other obstacles set up to safeguard investors from the unscrupulous, self-financing has been frowned on by lawyers and other professionals. Nevertheless, Smith & Hawken has been able to raise nearly $5 million without selling to a venture capital fund, going public, or paying someone else to do it. The total cost for raising funds has been slightly over $6,000, most of it legal fees, the rest airplane fares and coffee.

We have been able to do this for the following reasons.

1. We grew consistently and as predicted.
2. Investors were kept informed.
3. New investors were cultivated, by us and by other investors.
4. A market for the stock was created so that an investor could sell at any time he or she chose to.
5. There were no surprises, disappointments, or unkept promises.
6. We always raised money well in advance of need.
7. We had luck.

Leave even one out and the whole task of raising money privately becomes considerably more difficult.

CONSISTENT GROWTH

We started by selling $50,000 worth of stock at $2 per share, and a few months later we sold an equal amount. I didn't want to borrow, as I had done before, for three reasons. First, it's easier to stay in business if you don't owe anything. Second, I wanted patient money interested in long-term growth, because that's what I was aiming at. I didn't want investors who needed to "turn" their capital. Third, I wanted "permission" from investors not to make a profit for four years so that we could concentrate on making Smith & Hawken sound in management and systems.

In short, I wanted investors like my grandfather had been. A conservative executive fifty years ago, he thought then that he had made a pretty smart move when he earned 7 to 8 percent per year on an investment. In ten years, if he had earned back his original investment, he felt he had a good thing going. After all, the eleventh year was all gravy. Of course, my grandfather had that kind of rhythm and approach to life. He walked to his steel and cable company even though he was a vice president and could afford quicker means of transportation. He talked slowly and in measured terms. I suspect that he and his Masonic brethren who captained many of San Francisco's businesses acted pretty much the same.

You can't expect an investor in the 1980s to be happy with 7 to 8 percent for ten years, but you should avoid the investor who wants instant riches from your business. You want investors with my grandfather's attitude, updated of course for current rates of return.

I wanted patient money and I didn't want to lose a cent of it, so I made a deal with the early investors (of which I was the largest). While Dave Smith and I already had our founding stock, we would have options to buy an equal amount of stock as the original investors, on one condition: that we broke even for each of the first four years of the business. In other words, if we lost money, we lost our options. Dave and I, not the investors, set the conditions. But the conditions were more stringent than any investor would have dared to request.

How did we do? We barely made it. The first year, 1980, we did $40,000 in sales and broke even rather handily because we had no salaries, low rent, and few expenses other than tool and catalog costs. In the second year sales were $235,000 and breaking even became more difficult. Dave was starting to take some salary as he phased out of his other job, and we had to pay some employees. The third year, our mailing house (the people who sort the catalogs into bulk-rate bundles and take them to the post office) lost most of the catalogs in the fall only to rediscover them after Christmas. Coupled with a rising dollar that deflated our inventory value at year's end, breaking even was getting tortuously difficult. Year four marked $1.4 million in sales and a full-blown overhead, with Dave and me on full salary, a company vehicle, and even entertainment expenses. Not losing money that year was like trying not to make footprints in wet sand. Everywhere we stepped was a capital sink. The business was insatiably hungry for money. But we slipped by, aided in part by a legal settlement with the mailing house.

Sales were still climbing in our fifth year. At $2.4 million, our budgets had confidently predicted economies that would finally allow us to do better than break even. No one had told us about the mail order slough, the region between $1 and $4 million where most mail order catalog companies experience diseconomies of scale. Size becomes a temporary disadvantage. Orders, inquiries, and accounting demand sophisticated computer hardware and software, computer data processing skills, a programmer, semiautomated fulfillment machinery, and a telecommunications system (what we used to call phones, but since they're no longer cheap, they require an expensive name, too).

We didn't break even that year—a small loss, in fact—but we climbed out of that slough, and have made a profit ever since.

We have met or exceeded our sales goal every year, though. The net result of these eight years of steady growth is simple and obvious: if we say we will do something, investors and potential investors believe us. As I mentioned in the chapter on planning, business plans too often start with unrealistic projections designed to please investors. From the moment they open their doors these businesses are playing catch-up, trying to reach goals so unrealistic that they are abstract, and slowly eroding the credibility of the founders. Be consistent, realistic, honest, and forthright, and you will build investor confidence.

INFORMED INVESTORS

We keep our investors informed, not with the volume of information we produce, but with its accuracy. We talk with them over the telephone, in periodic meetings, and at an annual meeting. In a later chapter I will discuss straightforward, honest advertising, which is so rare these days that it delights the potential customer with its novelty. The same principle holds true for dealing with investors.

Honesty is a welcome surprise. Insight and candor about your company will assuage investor concerns and create interest. The more an investor knows about the company the more intelligently and enthusiastically he or she will discuss it with others. These discussions generate interest from new investors, while keeping earlier investors satisfied about the intelligence of their initial decision. One piece of information we shared on a timely basis was how the stock was doing. The price was going up.

CULTIVATING NEW INVESTORS

The grapevine works. We are constantly fielding inquiries regarding our stock. Is it for sale? How can I buy it? Because we have raised money on only three occasions following the initial capitalization, anyone wanting to buy stock has had to wait. During this waiting period, we kept potential investors as well informed as we did our current shareholders. If we didn't believe an individual would be a suitable shareholder, we dropped the contact.

As the time approached to raise more capital, I notified everyone six to twelve months in advance and set a price for the stock that seemed high at the time. But when the day came to issue the new shares, the price was usually more than reasonable, and the offering was sold out or oversubscribed.

CREATING A MARKET

Investors haven't wanted to wait for our official offerings, so anyone wanting to sell stock, including employees who had

145

been issued stock options, could sell anytime they wanted to. This was vitally important because the major problem facing investors in closely held companies is liquidity. What's the benefit if your investment has increased in value if you cannot get access to that appreciation? I own 10 percent of the stock in another company that I helped found in the late seventies. It now has revenues of over $10 million, but I might as well own China bonds. The stock has no market, no buyers, no value. It is meaningless unless the majority stockholder decides to sell or liquidate the business.

Because there is a market for Smith & Hawken stock, there are, ironically, very few sellers. They're not eager to sell because they know they can sell. Thus demand for the stock increases. Our last offer was $55 a share (as opposed to the original $2), and we sold $3.4 million worth. Even though the $55 was more than double the price of a few months prior, and even though we have had additional requests for approximately $1 million worth of stock, we cannot find a single shareholder who wants to sell his or her shares.

The liquid market for our shares has been equally important for employee compensation. It did not seem fair to issue stock options to employees unless each person had the sense that the stock would appreciate and be salable. Our stock option plan has meaning. Employees can calculate the value of their Smith & Hawken portfolio. One of our retail clerk's total compensation in 1986 came to nearly $50,000, counting profit sharing and stock appreciation. She may do even better in this year, 1987. When I mentioned this to another businessman, he asked me if this didn't bother me. To the contrary. It means we are exactly what we set out to be—a growing company.

NO SURPRISES

There have been surprises at Smith & Hawken, of course, but the shareholders have had no bad surprises. Anytime we have noticed a trend or change in the market, the need for a change in strategy, or any other detail that could ultimately result in a bigger problem, we have immediately notified our investors. The only way to maintain good shareholder relations is to hide nothing. The company is an open book. And if you take the lead with open communications, shareholders will not need to pester you. Remember, your job is not to sell the shareholders on your company. They are already sold. Your job is to treat them exactly as you treat a customer: inform, educate, and serve them.

RAISING MONEY IN ADVANCE

Ever try to borrow money when you were desperate? It's almost impossible. Your attitude drives people away. A visceral reaction to desperation may seem uncharitable or even heartless, but it is real. When raising money for your business, do so well in advance. I could easily repeat here my discussion about borrowing money: give yourself time to develop relationships. You want the investor to make an unhurried, confident decision. You want to avoid unnecessary stress. Raise money as you would run a long race—steadily, keeping pace.

LUCK

Luck, or serendipity, is earned. Luck does not mean that the whole world is out to do you good. Luck is working so hard at your craft, service, or enterprise that sooner or later you get a break. Luck or no, Smith & Hawken has had so many good breaks that we sometimes ascribe our fate to a great measure of good fortune. My wife asked me early on how the business was doing, and I replied that it seemed as if a guardian angel were hovering above us. Our timing was inadvertently perfect: the baby boomers were settling down, buying houses, and becoming interested in gardening. Perhaps because they are close to nature, gardeners turn out to be the most wonderful and kind customers a company could want. They are witty, forgiving, good-natured, and scrupulously honest.

Dave Smith once talked to a cataloger who specializes in electronic equipment, jewelry, exercise equipment, fancy watches, and high-tech gadgets. That company reported a 3 to 4 percent incipient fraud rate on credit card purchases. Asked what the Smith & Hawken rate was, Dave replied, "One." The guy was incredulous. Only 1 percent? No, Dave said. Only one bad transaction.

These customers have brought us investors who have been generous and unswervingly loyal. We could not have gone this far without them.

Know that raising equity capital is not as easy as I have

perhaps made it sound here. There are risks involved, and unless you are an experienced businessperson, you should not try to raise a million dollars after reading this or any other book. You will need a law firm, but be sure it is comfortable with this style of raising money—but not so comfortable it will charge you an arm and a leg. You can do most of the work yourself, with some prompting from your lawyers.

A variation on this do-it-yourself style of financing is provided by Ben & Jerry's, who came up with a free-spirited way to raise $750,000 that might be called "advanced bootstrapping." Their idea was simple and old but, in these modern times, rare. They did a self-registration for a stock offering in the state of Vermont. Instead of hassling with the Securities and Exchange Commission and New York investment bankers, they drew up their own prospectus and offered stock by advertising on the lid of the ice cream cartons and in local newspapers. "Get a scoop of the action" was the appeal, with an 800 number to call for a free offering. Believing that the community they worked in and that supported their product should benefit from their growth and profits, they made the minimum stock purchase as low as possible—just over $100. Their lawyers, advisors, accountants, and countless others said that a self-registration wouldn't work, that Vermont was too small, that it was too risky. It did work. They sold out the offering and in doing so assured themselves of many devoted customers. When the ice cream company went public with a stock offering on the over-the-counter market fifteen months later, the value of the original Ben & Jerry's shares tripled. Today, one out of every hundred families in Vermont owns Ben & Jerry's stock.

Growing a Business

No matter how you try to raise money—from friends, banks, the Small Business Administration, or investors—remember this one point that applies to all fund-raising situations: money goes to the least embarrassing situation.

The old saying is that money is invested or placed where it gets the highest return for the lowest risk. I say that money goes to where it causes the least embarrassment. People don't want to lose their money, but even more they don't want the humiliation, self-doubt, lack of esteem, or feeling of stupidity that goes with making a mistake. We are upset when we buy something that's useless; when we lend money and get burned; when an investment goes sour. First, we feel the loss of some quality of self; then we feel the loss of our capital and moan.

If you are fearful or grasping of money, your customer, the bank vice president, or the investor will spot this immediately, and the task of securing support will become immeasurably more difficult. In order to be a growing business and attract capital, you must project a sense that the world is expansive. Generosity, ampleness, and abundance draw money to ideas, people, and businesses. This is not a mandate for waste or glitzy promotion. It is simply knowing that your product or service touches a rich, fertile vein in the marketplace. In other words, have confidence in yourself and your business. This feeling will come through clearly in your dealings with people who have money, and they'll respond.

A successful retail store creates a secluded world unto itself. Compare Laura Ashley with a department store that has lost whatever sense of environment it might have had. How often does a wonderful store expand and thereby destroy the very environment that made it so appealing? When you expand, regardless of the type of business, never dilute the high compression of the experience you are creating.

Follow the lead of Banana Republic. Even after expansion, the founders of Banana Republic, Mel and Patricia Ziegler, cultivated a wonderful style in their catalogs, advertisements, and stores. They didn't sell clothes so much as tell stories with Mel's copy and Patricia's drawings. They sold adventure. Soon their customers and well-known personalities were passing along those stories. The Zieglers took generic clothing and made it fashionable because it was a direct manifestation of their own passion for travel and discovery. Their ideas and attention to detail are not gimmickry. They created a world that customers wanted to shop in, investors wanted to invest in, and, before long, The Gap wanted to buy.

Putting aside the monolithic corporations that succeed with sheer firepower, thriving businesses succeed because their founders give something to their customers more precious than money, something that is a part of themselves. We sense this, appreciate it, and, by becoming a customer, acknowledge and honor it.

8

The Lemonade
Stand

SOME PEOPLE cannot succeed in business no matter how hard they try. They buy a successful company and have it failing in no time. I know one of them, a friend with a brilliant mind and an unfailing sense of humor. He is energetic, hard working, and great with people, and he understands the peregrinations of the marketplace. He has been a publisher. He has started a school. He has been in the music, seed, and antiques businesses. Every venture has been an all-consuming dud. His friends marvel at his poor luck, misfortune, and bad timing. It seems unfair that he should not succeed when so many people of lesser skill do, but in fact there's a good reason for his failures.

Growing a Business

As a kid I worked as a waiter, dishwasher, packer, model, Christmas tree salesman, miner, and parts runner at an auto dealership. Over the years I began to realize that running a business does not require a brilliant mind. Some of my employers did quite well with modest minds, some with even less than that. But on the whole they were good businesspeople and I realized that another quality is more important than brainpower for running a business: "trade-skill," the most accurate term for the attribute I know of, coined by Michael Phillips and Salli Rasberry in their book *Honest Business*.

Tradeskill is really the set of skills that spell the difference between success and failure in a business. It is the knack of understanding what people want, how much they'll pay, and how they make their decision. It is knowing how to read the signals of the marketplace, how to learn from those signals, how to change your mind. Tradeskill gives you a canniness about how to approach a given product, market, or niche. (The geniuses of trade-skill are the turnaround "artists" who don't even need to "know" the business they are in. They perform radical, successful surgery on the patient simply by knowing what the disease is.) Tradeskill becomes a sixth sense that gives those who have it the ability to make decisions quickly, cutting through months of meetings, brainstorming, market studies, and bureaucratic shuffling. Tradeskill is knowing how to handle money, how to buy and how to pay.

While we recognize "natural" musical and athletic abilities, business ability, on the whole, is still considered something that you can acquire as an adult. But I believe tradeskill, like many skills, is easy to acquire when young, harder to get the knack of when you're older. Tradeskill is what you learn as a kid while running the paper route, working in your uncle's store, or starting an over-the-counter market in baseball cards. The smaller the business, the more important tradeskill becomes.

People with tradeskills are sometimes found at the very top of a corporation—often so in the garment business because it is extremely market sensitive—or at the "bottom," like the produce people in supermarkets. Tradeskills are demonstrated in abundance in the open-air wholesale produce and fish markets in New York and Hong Kong and every other big city. They are evident at horse and cattle auctions. They are almost never found in the middle management of oil companies, banks, insurance companies, or governments because these organizations are largely insensitive, even impervious, to subtle changes in the market.

Tradeskill cannot be learned from this or any other book. It is not for sale in the best M.B.A. programs in the country. Business education can be enormously deceptive to the student precisely because it obscures the need for tradeskill. Alice Medrich, founder of Cocolat, never perceived much relationship between her classroom work at business school and the small business she had started, almost unknowingly, in her kitchen. In fact, she was working on an informal proposal for a thesis on opening a small dessert shop while she was finding space for a shop and building tables. She realized she was more interested in doing it than writing about it—the ultimate thesis avoidance. Looking back after ten years, she sees some

155

value in business school, but she also knows that it gave her no vision or strength to get the job done.

Don't get me wrong. I would love to have had the opportunity to gain an M.B.A., because it is superb training in some areas of business. But if given the choice between the M.B.A. education or going to work at age twelve in order to support myself, I would choose the work experience as more valuable to a business education. As with money, too much "formal" business knowledge may be worse than too little for a small businessperson.

Most of us know whether we possess tradeskill. If you haven't got it—if you're uncomfortable haggling at a street market where the prices are negotiable, as an example, or if you're uncomfortable with strangers—the best thing to do is recognize this, just as you have recognized you're not a nuclear physicist, and plan your life and career accordingly. Going into business is not something to take lightly.

If you're thinking about starting a wholesale or retail business that requires a lot of interaction with people and money, and you believe you can substitute theoretical learning for the tradeskill you lack, beware. I recommend you not even try. Consider going into business with a partner who has it. If you don't feel comfortable conducting transactions with people, you should go to work for a business or individual and acquire tradeskills firsthand. Get behind the counter of a retail store, work with an entre-preneur, assist a business founder, or, if you are truly brave, work as a street vendor. Be sure that the job puts you in direct contact with both the customer and with organizing behind-the-scene tasks.

Am I suggesting that you quit your $30,000-a-year job in order to become a retail clerk before you open your pet store? No. I suggest you get a part-time job at night or on the weekends—consider it school—and find out how much you know. Don't underestimate the value of humility.

Because California is immodestly affluent in some places, there are many businesses started up by professionals from other fields, including many couples who worked for large corporations and set out on their own. The results of these businesses, usually retail stores, are sometimes painful to watch. Because the owners are well educated, well connected, well funded, and have "good taste," they believe they have the advantage over other merchants. They don't—unless they have tradeskill. We have all seen the food "shoppe" or toy boutique with the cute name, expensive custom-designed logo, well-chosen inventory, costly fixtures, beige carpets, and articulate help. Nice touches, but why does the shop feel dead? We as customers sense a lack of hands-on knowledge, authenticity, and market-sense. We want our businesses to be run by businesspeople, not by hobbyists. We're more comfortable in the hands of a pro than an amateur. Without tradeskill, a business seems a caricature of itself.

Michael Phillips and Salli Rasberry break tradeskill down into four specific attributes: persistence, the ability to face facts, the ability to minimize risk, and the ability to be a hands-on learner. I add a critical fifth criterion, the ability to grasp numbers. This is an arbitrary breakdown, but worthwhile for purposes of a detailed consideration of the subject. When just one of these skills is missing from a business, success will be considerably more difficult.

PERSISTENCE

Woody Allen said that 90 percent of success is showing up. Thomas Edison said that success is 10 percent inspiration and 90 percent perspiration. Winston Churchill said that "success is going from failure to failure with great enthusiasm."

I say that success can be avoided only if you try hard enough. From the day you start your company until the day you close it, sell out, or retire, being in business will be one long, continuing effort. Persistence is applying yourself doggedly and relentlessly to the daily tasks at hand, knowing there are no shortcuts. However, persistence does not require being bull-headed or overly aggressive. It does not require a Type A personality. Business persistence is a gentler quality, almost equine in its steadiness. We may lose sight of this because the business press is often guilty of describing companies and industries in terms of campaigns, victories, retaliations, and humbling defeats: business as war games, with the captains of industry setting strategy in their Lear jets. Journalists and their readers want the complexity of the commercial world reduced to this charade of someone winning, someone losing.

Such journalism belies the more pedestrian qualities that make companies winners, and foremost among these is persistence: never quitting, always trying, always working at the next problem. The Japanese are not conquering one worldwide industry after another with brilliantly executed sorties and ambushes. They're not spending a lot of time on the thrust and parry of takeover and acquisition. What they're doing is working hard at building, marketing, and servicing better products.

Business, like the economy itself, happens one step at a time, and it is the sum of these many steps—details, decisions, acts, and ideas—that becomes your company. If you're not in it for the long haul, your wish will come true.

FACING THE FACTS

At the heart of tradeskill is the ability to see events around you in a detached, pragmatic way. Starting or operating a business based upon the belief that the world is a certain way or should act in a certain way is unwise if not foolish. A seasoned businessperson never presumes to know "the truth," or believes that yesterday's truths are necessarily the truths of today. An experienced businessperson always asks questions. A green one will always have the answers.

In the 1950s, Gordon Sherman, the founder of Midas Mufflers, exalted a "ragtag bunch of garage mechanics, wrecking yard owners and parts dealers" into a group of muffler specialists, and tried to convince them that they were specialists not only because of what they did, but also because of what they did not do. Sherman believed that he was in the muffler business and only the muffler business. Business boomed, but out of this prosperity emerged an "evil influence": shock absorbers. Shocks were the mechanical equivalent of a muffler once the car was up on the rack—easy to diagnose, easy to install. Sherman discovered that his franchisees, bound by agreement to sell only mufflers, were bootlegging shock absorbers and hiding them when Sherman came around to inspect the premises. Even his friends among the Midas dealers were bootlegging the shock absorbers.

If Sherman opposed the shock absorbers too forcefully he could have laid himself open to antitrust suits, so he waged trench warfare against the shocks. The chain of franchises began to come apart. The dealers were willing to risk their franchises, very profitable franchises, in order to sell shocks. Sherman could not control the situation. He was up against a demiurge of the auto repair business, a force of "nature."

One morning he faced the fact that his dealers knew more than he did. He went on a closed-circuit broadcast to all the dealers and announced that forthwith Midas Mufflers would be adding shock absorbers to the line. He also announced a shock absorber sales contest with a trip to the Bahamas as first prize.

Some years later, a Midas dealer invented a $3,000 machine that allowed him to bend straight tubing into any of the several hundred different shapes required by a fully stocked dealer. He began a company to make and market the machine. Once again, Sherman's franchise agreement was threatened. He could have been wiped out by that machine because he was selling his franchisees finished mufflers and tailpipes. He faced that fact, too, and bought the company that was making the machine, then he asked every dealer who could afford to buy one to do so.

Another person I knew wasn't so good at facing the facts. He started a children's toy and clothing company after he had built up a very successful adult clothing company which he had sold to a national chain. He plunged right back into business with considerable cash and confidence.

The children's clothing sold in his store was expensive, the carpet thick, and the fixtures deluxe. Rather than projecting an image of children as wondrous, squealing, and delightful, his store and literature created an image of a child who was upwardly mobile, striving to get ahead, and awkwardly image conscious. His company literature showed small children dressed as preppies—six-year-olds in blazers and rimless glasses.

He had chosen outstanding toys, games, and computer software, but the preppie image he was touting made many parents avoid his business. From the start, traffic in his downtown San Francisco store was sparse. His mail order catalog did only slightly better. He had based the store on the idea that the baby boomers were having fewer children, later in life, and would spend more on them, but the sales failed to confirm this viewpoint. His friends and associates tried as graciously and politely as possible to tell him why they thought the approach was inappropriate and should be changed, but no one could dissuade him. Instead of facing the facts, he tried harder, borrowed more money, and dug a deeper hole. Persistence without facing the facts will lead you astray.

One of Smith & Hawken's competitors also failed to face the facts. When we were two years old, one of our domestic suppliers decided that we were selling so many of their tools that they would also market directly to the customer, bypassing us and coming out with their own catalog. But while they believed they were "competing" with us, we expanded our line to the point that tools comprised only 20 percent of our sales. My partner Dave Smith and I had realized that our customers were gardeners, certainly, but that tools were not necessarily their main interest. We even changed our name from Smith & Hawken Tool Co. to simply Smith & Hawken, and we added a subtitle on the cover of our catalog reading CATALOG FOR GARDENERS. These seemed like small enough changes, but they were vital. The competitor never figured out that the market had changed, or that it had never been what it appeared to be. After struggling for four years and losing money, they went out of business in 1986. I believe that the owner had not faced up to the fact that his tools were overbuilt, over-priced, and overmarketed (he sent too many catalogs to the wrong people). He was able to last as long as he did only because he had started with a lot of money and could cover the losses. (Yet another danger of having too much money: you will face the facts too late.)

The inability to face the facts is not limited to small businesses. General Motors still has not faced the fact that its cars are poorly made, that its dealer network does not understand customer service, or that in the late 1980s it is trying to sell its customers the technological equivalent of a 1979 Toyota. In fact, the bulk of American companies have not faced up to the fact that most of their customers feel badly treated, that most American workers do not feel respected by management, and that virtually all of our industries will be hit by foreign competition. Like a terrible family secret, American companies have not yet compre-hended, much less explained, that in order for our economy to thrive, there will have to be a revolution in how we relate to each other as people, co-workers, and customers. In starting your own business, observe well how refusal to face the facts results in economic loss.

MINIMIZING RISKS

I have said that the image of entrepreneurs as risk-takers is mostly journalism. The purpose of business is not to take risks. The idea, rather, is to get something done. Risk is inherent in a venture, but entrepreneurship should not be equated with risk-taking. There is risk in driving an automobile but a good driver does everything possible to mitigate it—fastening the seat belt, observing the speed limit, heeding warning signs, staying sober, and more. A person with tradeskill will continually look at his business the same way. He will identify the risks, and work down the list so that every potential concern has been addressed in some manner.

A good business is almost organic in the way it comprises redundant systems and backups to handle the unexpected. In staffing, you should cross-train so the business is not dependent on any one person, particularly yourself. In finance, you should avoid any strategy that could bring the company down with just a single misstep. Early Winters, a Seattle-based outdoor clothing and equipment company, grew to $14 million in sales under the tutelage of its three founders. But they were stretched so thin financially that one bad season sent them into bankruptcy. Twelve years of hard work were lost in a matter of months simply because they had not sufficiently capitalized the business earlier.

At this writing I am adding bulbs from Holland, Israel, Oregon, and Japan to Smith & Hawken's line. Two hundred varieties, and I don't have a clue as to which bulbs will be favored by our customers. In this branch of the business I am as wet and green as I can be, and we will make serious mistakes in inventory projections. On the other hand, we're sure the business is there; we have sold bulbs every year in our retail stores. So how do we balance the requirement of having enough bulbs with the risk of having far too many? Unlike our tools, the bulbs don't last forever in the warehouse.

For each of the past five years we have had one or two "seconds sales" at our warehouse, attended by thousands who benefit from great bargains and discounts, the horticultural equivalent of Filene's Basement. My plan on the bulbs is to over order. If we order way too many, we can hold a seconds sale featuring bulbs at virtually the lowest prices in California, since we will be a direct importer. We won't lose money (we won't make any, either), our customers will have had a fantastic sale, our mail order customers will have received what they wanted, and we will have learned what we need to know to order intelligently the next season.

Our risks are minimized.

HANDS-ON LEARNERS

When I was between businesses, I decided to get involved with a few turnarounds for companies that had failed or gone bankrupt. Most companies in bankruptcy are a pleasure to work with. It's remarkable how receptive to change people are after their businesses have failed. In one case, however, the owner could not learn that his business was failing, and would continue to do so, simply because he wasn't a hands-on learner. He was there but he wasn't there.

He had founded a company that made insoles for running and tennis shoes. It was a modest endeavor with an equally modest market. He began it with high hopes, two dozen investors, an office, a staff, a big oak desk, salespeople, and even a few consultants. From day one, the founder got behind that desk and ran the company— eventually into the ground. He sat there and dictated memos, answered letters, conducted meetings, and talked to his far-flung sales representatives. He worked hard, accomplished a little, and by the end of the first year he had spent all of the paid-in capital, he had no inventory, his sales were declining, and his demoralized staff had not been paid in months.

The image of an executive moored behind his desk is almost absurd in a business that does less than $50 million a year. Up to that point, there is simply no reason why any person, much less the founder, should not be in touch with all aspects of the business, learning from his or her own experience rather than by memo, E-mail, or committee.

It is true that in very successful companies hands-on involvement can pose a conflict in the transition from an entrepreneurial company to a managerial company—the difficulty of Apple Computer in making the transition is a notorious recent example. But don't worry about some future management stage for your business while you're still struggling with the entrepreneurial problems. Unless the business you are doing is one you have done before, anything less than total attention to all aspects of the company foretells problems. Keep in mind that you cannot delegate what you do not understand. You probably won't be able to sell it, either.

WORKING WITH NUMBERS

As you read this book, you are not reaching for a dictionary every other sentence. When you read the numbers of a business, you shouldn't have to reach for a calculator every other line. Numbers are a logic and a language. There is binary logic (used in computers), everyday logic, and numeral logic. You need at least the last two to move and act in commerce.

Numbers express relationships. Any business, whether manufacturing, service, or retail, consists of hundreds and thousands of relationships that can be expressed, analyzed, and conceptualized through numbers. Many people in business with little or no education or training nevertheless succeed—in good part because they have an intuitive sense of these numbers.

For the first seven years of my business career, I was at the mercy of my bookkeeper. She was oracular, and I waited nervously and anxiously for the close of every month's P&L. It took about fifteen years before I actually understood the double-entry method of accounting. Not bragging, mind you, but as much as I pretended to read, understand, and comment on profit-and-loss statements and balance sheets, there was a thick film of ignorance which I was too embarrassed to admit.

The numbers that I will be talking about here are not those profit-and-loss numbers, or not in complete detail. It is precisely because you may not be an expert in accounting that you should "internalize" your bookkeeping methods. Business is the school of the practical, and nothing is more practical than knowing the flow of money in and out.

"Creative accounting" has become a term for cooking your books with technicalities that are quasi-acceptable to auditors and the IRS. Too bad, because truly creative accounting is the ability to understand what is happening inside your business before seeing the books at the end of the month, quarter, or year. You must be able to sense the numbers like you sense your toes and fingers. I have a friend who can do this so well that, when the accountant brings the profit-and-loss statement for the close of the prior month, he can glance at it and tell within seconds whether it is right or wrong. He does this despite the fact that he has not looked at the actual books all month long. This is not brilliance, intuition, or voodoo. It is simply a result of his never forgetting the essential ratios and relationships of his business. He keeps a running tally in his head all month long and knows within plus or minus 5 percent what the results will be.

Business is composed of two streams of money—the money coming in and the money going out. A good accounting system built into your business and your head will convey to you easily and quickly the relationship of the monies within each stream, and the relationship between the two streams.

Spending money, whether on rent, shelves, copy machines, or a lathe, is the beginning of your books. Recognize these expenditures as pump priming. Energy has to go out before it will come in. This is the time to know every detail of how it is spent. Do not delegate to consultants and experts. When you are starting up, money can only go out for a period of time. Even seasoned pros do not know exactly how customers will respond. Neither will you. A simple rule of thumb is this: the more experience you have in business, the more money you can spend on a new business. Conversely, the less experience, the less initial money that should be spent.

Once revenues begin to come in, you should construct a way to know roughly but accurately what your daily flow of cash is. And from that point on, you should know at any given time how much cash you have on hand, how much cash is coming in on a daily, weekly, and monthly basis, and how much money is going out. Finally, you should know how much money you owe or are owed. These figures should sleep with you like toy teddies and you should be able to grasp them out of thin air like the date of your birthday. The only way to learn this is to start when the business begins. And never stop doing it.

The relationship between the two streams, money in and money out, is pivotal. When money in exceeds money out, it is profit. As Peter Drucker stated most clearly: profit is a cost of doing business. You need it in order to grow.

The Springfield Remanufacturing Center in Missouri operates under the novel belief that every employee—there are about 350 people—must know the numbers. The Great Game of Business at SRC wouldn't be fair if the employees didn't know the rules, and the rules are the numbers. Every department at SRC functions as a small business, with managers and supervisors establishing budgets after consultations with the workers in that department. SRC employees understand income statements, cash flow analyses, inventory controls, materials flow, and basic accounting. Depending on the analysis selected, daily, weekly, monthly, or yearly figures are related to the job performance of the employee, department, and entire shop. Before their education in accounting began, few of the employees knew even the basics of pretax profits and retained earnings. Now they understand all the accounting behind these figures—and this understanding contributes to the profits.

Whatever your business, you the owner certainly have to grasp the essential number relationships. Further, in every business there is a "model" relationship between sales and expenses. Over the years, experience has taught your peers what this model relationship is, what can be achieved in terms of costs and revenues and what cannot or should not. This is conventional wisdom, yes, but the wisdom of businesspeople, not of business schools. Find out what it is. In *The Entrepreneur & Small Business Problem Solver* by William A. Cohen, there is a listing of the trade associations in the United States and Canada. Most of these groups publish studies of their field that show the financial relationships as established historically. Also listed in his book are five other sources for business ratios. (The book is invaluable in countless other ways— probably the single most helpful book for someone starting a business.)

In my consulting days, I was brought in by a small group that had started a greengrocer and corner store in a major city. It was a big success—plenty of customers—but it was losing money. They wanted to know why. Everything in the books looked normal except for labor cost, which was 18 percent of revenues. The owners didn't know that specialty food retailing can't make a profit if labor exceeds

10 percent of income. They cut their labor costs and have been profitable ever since.

Once you know what these important ratios or relationships should be in your business (for the greengrocer, $10 in for every $1 out to employees), you can track them daily or weekly. No need to wait for the bookkeeper. Further, once you know what ratios are "possible," they are easier to achieve.

In the catalog business, approximately eight thousand different companies vie for your mailbox. When Smith & Hawken started, someone mentioned a simple rule: the cost of goods and the cost of the catalog and any associated advertising, excluding labor, could not exceed 70 percent of revenue. Simple ratio, and true enough as a guide. Because I know this ratio and know my weekly labor costs, I know that Smith & Hawken breaks even at sales of $43,000 per day, as of this writing. Of course there is tremendous fluctuation day to day, and weeks of actual losses in the fall when business is slow. No ratio can change these fluctuations, but knowing the numbers on a daily basis and tracking how they change assures me that the books are at my disposal, and ready for use.

Your business should maintain a daily log of its activities. No matter how large the business, these numbers are always crucial. If you log them consistently, you won't go crashing into icebergs in the fog, nor will this information sink into the deep recesses of the accounting or bookkeeping department only to emerge weeks or months later in a less comprehensible form. We have been doing a daily log at Smith & Hawken from the time we started. Our log consists of the following categories.

REVENUES

This shows how many orders came in by mail, how many by phone, and how each of the two stores did. These figures are entered every day as soon as the mail is opened or, in the case of phone orders, the next day when the orders have been processed by the computer. We know the size of the average mail and phone order. We also catalog institutional or bulk sales as they occur. At the end of the week, the columns are totaled and overall averages calculated. Under each column of revenue figures for mail, phone, and store is the comparable figure for the same week of the two prior years. This comparison helps our planning, staffing, prediction, and analysis.

CATALOGS MAILED

We mail six different catalogs on thirty-five different weeks of the year, in varying quantities. These numbers are logged and matched against prior years. Since we mail at pretty much the same times every year, we can create a simple column comparing the number of catalogs mailed to the revenues received. In other words, if we mail 50 percent more spring catalogs, and revenues are up 53 percent, we know this catalog is more "efficient" than the one the year before. This is a critical ratio for us to watch. And we watch it every week.

CASH BALANCE

Knowing your daily balance is checkbook stuff, except many businesses don't do it. Our version is a simple page with columns showing cash received each day, disbursements out, and cash on hand. It also shows money transferred to our account from the bank and any money owed on our floating line of credit.

PAYROLL

Our logs show payroll by department ("warehouse, administrative, customer service, retail stores #1 and #2, etc.") as a percentage of gross revenues for that bimonthly period. The payroll also shows the same figures for the previous year, so we can see whether specific departments or the overall company is getting more or less efficient. This prevents midriff bulge.

CUSTOMER SERVICE

Our customer service log shows how many phone and mail inquiries came in for one day and by the week. It shows how many requests or returns were processed, and how many, if any, are more than one or two days old. On the same page we show revenues and orders received, so we can compute a quick rate-of-returns figure. Most mail order companies run from 4 to 6 percent on returns. We try to keep our returns under 1 percent.

These are the main logs, but there are many others. We log phone orders by time of day received, top fifty products by category and price, nursery sales as a subset of retail, total packages shipped, unfilled orders at end of day, number of orders shipped partially, number of back orders for day, week, cumulatively, and so on. The computer handles the heavy lifting.

If the logs are slightly off it doesn't matter, because they are not the accounting work sheets. They are the compasses. They tell us at a glance, all of us, where we are and where we might be veering slightly from course, and they give us information quickly enough so we can do something about the situation before it becomes a problem.

From experience at Smith & Hawken, we know to the day when phone orders will spurt following the shipment of our catalog, and then when the mail orders will begin to come in. In November 1986, we had directed the shipping house to delay shipment until after the elections (standard procedure in the mail order business because people are distracted during the week prior to the election). Our "drop" was timed to hit right after Election Day. But on the day we were expecting increased orders to start coming in, nothing happened. Our logs revealed how far short of previous years' orders we were. The next day we called the mailing office to see whether the catalogs were mailed on time. No, they weren't mailed on time, we were told, but they would arrive on time. But the numbers got worse each day. Either people weren't responding to our Christmas catalog, or the catalogs had not in fact been mailed. We demanded postage receipts and when we finally received them, we learned that there had indeed been a ten-day delay in mailing the catalogs. Now we knew that we would have a very sharp peak in telephone orders and we had to reschedule to prepare for it. We also had to pay about $40,000 in second-day air charges to assure arrival of some merchandise by Christmas but these expenses were reimbursed by the printing company. Without the logs, the affair would have been even worse because we wouldn't have known what to anticipate or how to get things straightened out.

9

If You Meet the Buddha on the Road, Sell Him

T HE MARKET is as much a part of your company as you are. After all, it represents one-half of the ledger. To grow, your business must earn the permission of the marketplace. No concept is more important for the start-up entrepreneur. The customer must give your business permission to sell to him. He does this (at least as a repeat customer) only after a thorough assessment of you, your product or service, and your operation. This is why Detroit is having trouble selling cars even though they're better built than they were. These cars have to overcome years of bad notices. It will take time to accomplish this. In fact, it may take until there's a complete turnover in the market—

until those of us who now think Japanese or German no longer drive.

If you're starting out in business you have a grace that you can always keep. If you start with quality and the truth you'll never have to stop. There will be no reason to. But once you stop telling customers the truth—or don't tell the truth from the beginning—you will find it's difficult to start later. The value of honesty, like virginity, lies in its irreplaceability. I'm not talking about image, either. I am talking about what's genuine. You become what you say, and what you say becomes you.

In order to develop a good business idea and earn the permission of the marketplace, you must *be* the market. You should want to shop at the store you run or receive the services you offer. Every expression of the business—its ads, decor, service, packaging, pricing, and selling techniques—should be 100 percent credible, respectable, and acceptable to you.

Permission of the marketplace is many times more important than capital. American businesses spend $95 billion every year assaulting our sensibilities with their ads. Many of these ads try to bludgeon the marketplace into cooperating, and it's possible to do that with enough money and certain kinds of products, such as soft drinks and detergents, which are so vacuous they offer the customer no meaningful choice.

American marketing has been a centrifugal system wherein goods are pushed out from the center of big business to the farthest margins of the consumer society. In Japan and, indeed, in any truly effective marketing system of worthwhile goods, the effort is centripetal. Rather than

RESTAURANT - BAR
SLAMMERS - BAR

THE BEST
MEXICAN FOOD

TEX MEX

SEA FOOD AMERICAN CUTS

CRISANTEMAS No. 10

PHONE 4-21-05   CANCUN, Q. ROO

Laura

LA POSTA

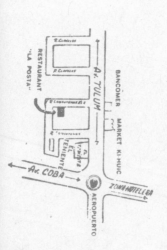

goods being pushed, needs are *drawn out* of the customer and *into* the business, and then fulfilled. This does not call for reading the customer's mind or doing surveys. More important is to watch the customer's hands, eyes, feet, and body. See what people do and don't do, the attractions and repulsions, and observe the minutiae of daily life so that you can say before the buyer even knows it, "This is what you want." This is what we try to do with our Smith & Hawken gardening catalog.

We are all increasingly surfeited with advertisements and have become skeptical of the hard sell. We know we can be tempted as consumers, but we don't want ads to pander to this weakness. Such ads remind us of the endless consuming spiral we seem to be locked into, but as customers, not consumers, we prefer a genuine and different approach.

Carl Schmitt at the University National Bank in Palo Alto understands that the public has learned to disregard bank ads about service. Every bank advertises its good service, but very few actually deliver it. So UNB doesn't even try to overcome that built-in skepticism. One ad announces UNCOLA BANKING above a picture of a vanity license plate stamped UNBANK. Below the picture is copy that begins: "Exactly what it says. *Un*common, *un*derstated, *un*like any other bank you've ever dealt with." Another ad asks, "Is your banker's head screwed on right?" The drawing shows a pin-striped banker whose head is facing backward.

Most of what has been written on marketing is based on considerations of what the customer is *supposed* to want and *supposed* to think. The moment you go into business marketing products to a supposition, you're lost. Tom Peters writes in his "search for excellence" series about the need to stay close to the customer, which is a clear way of expressing the timeless business adage of providing the customer with a good product at a fair price. That axiom is certainly true, but I believe there's a clearer way yet to think about this key to all business success. While you can "approximate" the customer, you can only know yourself. So stay close to the person you understand, and market products for yourself. This takes the guesswork out of it.

When starting your business, you will be starting out with limited resources and quite likely dealing with a new product or wrinkle. Take your time. There's plenty of it. If you try to rush your message and do and say too much, you'll create cynicism, in your customers and yourself. Don't make the mistake of believing you get only one chance to reach your potential customer, or believing that each package or advertisement must tell everything. Much better is to proceed as though you are having a long dialogue with your customer. Let your ads have the expansiveness of a friendship. Write copy that respects this relationship. It might take longer to make your first sale to a customer, but that first sale won't be the last one.

Don't even think about barging into the marketplace alongside K mart. Forget the full-color ads (you won't be able to afford them anyway) and any other marketing campaign that feigns bigness. You're not big. Your market doesn't want big. If it wants big and you're not able to deliver big, you have the wrong business going. If you're marketing a product to a customer who knows the product area, she will recognize that you are the new kid on the block. Don't break down the customer's front door with bold-face type. Let her discover you.

You'll have to appeal to your prospective customers' common sense and intelligence. Start with small, imaginative forays into promotion—small ads in a trade magazine, a hang tag on your bottle of salad dressing, simple, straightforward copy on your label, or a good brochure. Remember, a useful product is not that hard to sell. Start slowly and let the customers come to you. Customers enjoy discovering new things. These are the items they mention around town. Despite all those huge ads posted by the movie companies, they know very well that one and one factor only sells tickets: word-of-mouth.

Ben Cohen and Jerry Greenfield had a different idea from their main competitors—the deluxe ice creams—about how to market the product. Häagen-Dazs is a meaningless term in a nonexistent language, a made-up word that sounds foreign. The Häagen-Dazs package shows an outline of Scandinavia, but the ice cream is made in New Jersey. Frusen Glädjé is another meaningless term, a company started up as a knockoff of Häagen-Dazs (these companies are now owned by Kraft and Pillsbury, respectively).

Ben and Jerry created a hand-lettered container with their pictures on the top, a cow on the side, and Vermont-made ice cream inside. Real people selling real ice cream with natural ingredients—with the clearly stated exception of the Heath bars and Oreo cookies.

In the case of *Harrowsmith* magazine, Jim Lawrence mailed 15,000 copies of his first issue free to subscribers of *Harrowsmith*'s competitor, *Organic Gardening,* a practice almost unheard of in marketing a new magazine. Subscription solicitations operate on the assumption that people subscribe to find out what's in a new magazine when they know very little. Lawrence ignored the conventional marketing wisdom. More than 20 percent of those who received a free copy subscribed.

Smith & Hawken is in a mail order business that sends out unsolicited catalogs. When you start out in this business, one of the first things to investigate is what sort of appropriate mailing lists exist in your field. A new company's first catalogs are usually sent to the names on anywhere from 25 to 100 different lists, 125,000 to 500,000 names in all. The results are analyzed and the lists that "performed" are rolled out into larger mailings. This is the "science" of direct marketing that distributes the 40 billion pieces of mail we throw away the moment they drop through the chute.

Smith & Hawken decided not to rent a single name for our first four years of operation. Instead, we placed small ads in magazines involved with horticulture and gardening, and in a few magazines with a large number of homeowners as subscribers.

As for a catalog, I knew only that I didn't like what was around. I didn't appreciate copy that made me feel my life would be bereft if I didn't buy an electronic mail detector for my rural mailbox, a set of Golden Retriever–embellished cocktail tumblers, or my very own high-frequency rodent repeller. Most catalogs addressed me as if my desires had overwhelmed my IQ years ago. I didn't like all the come-ons about discounts and the "surprise gift" to be included with my order, or photography so overdone that the actual product looked a little tawdry when it finally arrived. And then there were the 800 numbers that reached a contract phone service clerk who knew absolutely nothing about the products I was ordering. In short, those catalogs addressed me as a consumer rather than as a potential customer.

The few exceptions—White Flower Farm, L. L. Bean, Norm Thompson, Brookstone (before it was bought out by The Quaker Oats Co. and later sold)—seemed like old-fashioned companies with unalloyed virtues predating the era of specialty retailing, "niche" marketing, and market segmentation.

Smith & Hawken came later, so our job was to figure out what kind of company we would be in the brave new world of retailing. The answer was simple. We would be a catalog *we* would buy from. We would not use color (in the beginning), we would not attend seminars on how to make a million in direct mail, we would not hire consultants, read trade publications, join the Direct Marketing Association, use a fulfillment house, have a contracted twenty-four-hour 800 number, rent lists, or have a catalog house design our "image." As a friend said at the time, our plan might not have been intelligent, but at least it was stubborn.

Our first mailing was 487 catalogs (from which we eventually received 283 orders). That list grew only as we added the names of people who had purchased from us or inquired about our business. All those tiny ads kept registering quietly in people's minds. They didn't amount to much in themselves, but their persistence proved that we were still around and still doing business. People began to wonder, *Well, what are these tools?* Slowly, ever so slowly, our list grew and so did our revenues. It was slow going, but we gained authenticity and staying power.

After four years of operation, we had a house file of 200,000 names at Smith & Hawken. We were ready to rent our first list from the outside. We were "cold-calling," yes, but many people had read or heard about us, so we weren't unknown. The mailing was accepted—it produced good results. About a year later, Brookstone, by then a division of Quaker Oats, passed the word in the trade that they were going to create a catalog that would dent our sales. Why not? Brookstone had been in the mail order business for twenty years, they sold tools, some of them garden related, they had a professional team of buyers and marketers, and they had one of the best fulfillment operations in the mail order business (that is, they mailed orders out fast). They had by our estimate 400,000 mail order customers, we had 25,000. We had done the legwork in the field, now they would come in and walk off with the prize. We must have looked like a sitting duck.

Their catalog was tested under three different names and mailed to 1 million customers. It didn't work. Brookstone didn't have the permission of the marketplace. Zeal, experience, and money are no substitute. At the beginning of this book, I wrote that I had no intention of trying to tell you how to make a killing in business because proceeding with that idea of quick wealth in mind is a fatal error. A "killing" has nothing to do with *growing* a business.

No company has stronger permission from the market-place than L. L. Bean of Freeport, Maine. On top of excellent products and service, they were the fortunate beneficiaries of the trend toward preppiness in the late seventies. Bean became the vendor of choice for a whole generation. The company could have played to this trend, but they wisely chose to stay with their original identity. They deliberately held back growth for two years and rededicated themselves to outdoor sporting goods. They didn't let the success go to their heads, and they believe this caution saved the company.

In one minor way, however, Bean may have slipped up. The Bean label, which had always been an "inside" label, suddenly appeared on denim jeans and wristwatches on the outside. I'm not privy to Bean's sales (the company is privately held), so I don't know whether these products succeeded. I know that to me and some friends with whom I discussed those blue jeans, Bean might have overstepped the implicit agreement that bound the company and the customer. The Bean customer isn't interested in designer labels. That label on the jeans didn't seem right.

Patagonia mail order continues to earn permission from the marketplace with copy that is witty, humorous, playful and extremely accurate. The following piece, used to describe some of its travel clothes, was written by Nora Gallagher and Yvon Chouinard:

> Travel clothes have always been a disaster. Made of shiny synthetics and weird knits, they have always bestowed on travellers the awful *nom*, "tourist." To avoid even the suggestion of such a reputation, people will go to great lengths; the result is that they look like something the cat dragged in when they arrive in foreign

hotels. Wrinkled Oxford shirts; heavy, hot blue jeans; blazers sodden and undone. If they look bad, they feel worse. And if their destination is any country south of San Francisco or west of Hawaii, they will be sure to be sweltering and disheveled by the second cup of morning tea.

We offer shirts for both men and women, trousers and a split skirt for women who must maneuver both foreign customs and foreign terrain. The money belts we make are classic, leather belts that will safely stash your cash whenever you travel among pickpockets, inflationary conditions, and American Expressless hotels. Last, but certainly not least, we designed a sport coat that can travel anywhere without ruining your good name. We call it our Travel Tweed.

Imagine if you were sailing around the world or climbing Mount Everest, you would need a sport coat for the Royal New Zealand Yacht Club or for the embassy party after the climb. It shouldn't have mildewed or gotten moth eaten in the hold, and it should come out of the pack relatively wrinkle free.

This excellent, classic jacket is the cornerstone of Patagonia's Travel Line: practical clothing that goes from portages to palaces with equal aplomb. Other people have made wrinkle-free sport coats, but they always turned out so ugly as to be unwearable. We have searched the world for the perfect material and finally settled on a Japanese made polyester tweed. It looks nothing like a polyester, has a soft hand and comes in a brown tweed color that goes well with dress khakis or Levis.

The Travel Tweed coat has a skeleton lining of tough, ripstop nylon which won't grow ragged with wear or easily tear on a kayak or Bombay taxi. Its inside pockets are oversized to accommodate passports and maps; there

184

is an outside chest pocket. Two flap covered pockets at the lower front provide ample space into which one may shove one's fists when posing over newly ratified treaties or freshly made gins and tonic.

Instructions for folding the coat (essential for it to reach its full potential) are woven and sewn into the inside breast pocket so you won't lose them in the flight. The coat comes with its own ripstop travel pouch (11″ × 11″ × 1″), to protect it from becoming soiled in your pack. We don't guarantee this coat to be 100% wrinkle free, but at worst you may have to hang it up in the bathroom while you shower so the wrinkles hang out. Dry clean only. Imported.

That's a pretty long statement but I don't believe you became bored with it. From the first sentence the copy establishes a rapport with you, the prospective buyer, and it never lets you down.

Hemingway once said that every writer needs a 100 percent built-in, shock-proof crap detector. If this is all that a writer needs, this country is full of them, because most American consumers have developed an effective crap detector. The more sophisticated the techniques of Madison Avenue, the more sophisticated our discernment. We may buy junk at times, but we know it's junk that suits our trivial purpose, or else it's all we can afford. (Those ads for Hondas and Toyotas are not selling the cars. Our past experience with the cars is selling the cars.)

As a new businessperson, try to be authentic in your presentations to the marketplace. In a way, the junk ads are a boon to the honest, no-nonsense marketer. Honest copy and ads come across as refreshing change: we immediately recognize the authenticity and are disarmed. Thus, marketing is easier than ever before. Simply be up front with your customer and tell him what *you* want to know.

Even in a competitive situation, honesty and frankness can be far more effective than glitz, promotion, and hype. Ben & Jerry's reached a turning point in their business when Pillsbury purchased competitor Häagen-Dazs. Pillsbury apparently put pressure on distributors to remove Ben & Jerry's from their product line. Although their first thought was to sue, they realized that a court case would drag on for years, be very costly, and might result in their near-term bankruptcy. So they started a bumper sticker campaign that ballooned into their most successful "marketing" campaign. It started off with Jerry standing in front of Pillsbury with a picket sign that said, "What's the Doughboy Afraid Of?" Then came the bumper stickers with the same message. Then the ads in buses, and even an airplane to fly a banner around. They put an 800 number on the carton of their ice cream with the same phrase, "What's the Doughboy Afraid Of?" People calling got a recorded message from Jerry describing their plight with Pillsbury. He would ask them to leave their name and address and he would send them a Doughboy kit. The kit was a further explanation, bumper stickers, and two letters for the customer to sign and send. One was a letter of complaint to Pillsbury, the other was to the State Attorney General in Vermont. Publicity mounted. The media jumped on the story. A hundred calls a day came into the office supporting Ben and Jerry. Finally, Pillsbury relented, and Ben & Jerry's was back on the shelf next to Häagen-Dazs, only now with enormous exposure and publicity. Ben and Jerry see it as the turning point in their growth and development.

As a small businessperson, you have no greater leverage than the truth. I am not referring to the gimmick of admitting you're number two, so therefore you're trying harder. I mean outright disclosure to the customer of the quality and nature of your products and services. In the tawdry world of braggadocio, the truth rings with clarity.

Consider this frank admission of error to its customers from White Flower Farm:

> In the spring edition of *Garden Book,* we apologized for our inability to transfer incoming calls from the old telephone order number to the new one. The problem was caused by the October installation of a phone system whose technology seemed to exceed our grasp. Our agony was bliss compared to the later discovery that between November and late March countless calls went unanswered because the ringing heard by you was not heard by us. Yes, we were there. In fact, we rather wondered what had become of you. Once the malfunction was discovered, the phone company removed the entire system and replaced it with something less advanced but more reliable. In the meantime, many friends received shabby treatment at our hands, for which we are very sorry. Calls now receive the kind of prompt attention you would expect. Makes one long for the old monopoly.

Another way to look at honesty in marketing is as a change in the "signal to noise ratio"—information theory applied to the marketplace. The noise is the $95 billion spent on advertising and promotion, the market equivalent of all the city sounds we tune out in self-defense. The signal is the clear tone of honesty that comes through in the

187

market as compellingly as the siren of an ambulance. The ambulance has no choice other than screaming louder than everything else in order to be heard. You can and should accomplish the same goal by conducting your conversation with the customer in a calm and easy tone.

In early 1986 the House of Representatives was voting on an aid package to the Nicaraguan contras. Right-wing supporters of that cause spent $2 million on television in their lobbying effort. For months there was no advertising from the other side of the issue. Then a San Francisco group, the Public Media Center, ran a one-page ad in *The New York Times* two days before the contra vote. Over a paragraph describing contra atrocity ran the headline: WHEN IT COMES TO TERRORISM, YOU GET WHAT YOU PAID FOR. Readers were asked to call or telegraph their Congresspersons. The bill was defeated and many people credit that $20,000 newspaper ad that cost 1 percent of the expenditure of the pro-contras.

The market is a stream of information constantly flowing into your business. Once you sense the stream and are able to read its signals, your business is born—and you know it. This is the moment you are searching for. The feeling is like gliding, skiing, or any other sport in which your body may feel almost transcendent. Business isn't a sport, but that feeling is visceral, not intellectual. When you and your business are in the center of the market, like a sculler you will feel the quiet strength of the pull on your shell.

At Erewhon we started out as absolute food geeks: our foods were so outside the mainstream that people couldn't pronounce the names of half of them. We were treated with suspicion or derision. A trucker unloading some millet asked us who ate the bird food.

With most businesses, the idea is to establish a niche in the existing market for their product. But to establish a business with products that are novel, you must in effect create a new market. You're competing not against other products but against the inertia of the marketplace. It is one thing to come out with a new ice cream; it is another entirely to market tofu-based ice cream substitutes. Given equally good products, the ice cream maker will have an easier time than the tofu maker.

In the case of Erewhon, we knew we had located the center of the stream in the food business in 1970 or so, when natural food stores were opening as quickly as they could line up vendors. By then we had added a wholesale operation to our retail business, and we landed a hundred new accounts a month. On top of expanded resales, our list of new customers was increasing almost exponentially. In fact, many of the new stores were being opened by our former customers.

At Smith & Hawken we started out in 1980 with the princely sum of $40,000 in sales. We were not noticed. But as we began to grow we realized that we would exhaust our initial customer base, gardeners who were passionately involved in horticulture and reveled in the nature of our tools and other products. There weren't that many of them. To grow, we would have to break out from that smaller base without losing it or our identity and originality.

When we reached $2 million in sales we seemed on the verge of reaching that broader audience, but then we were hit with an onslaught of competition—from one company to eight, almost overnight, and some were well financed and knowledgeable. For the next eighteen months, our initial customer base was deluged with knockoffs and knockoffs of knockoffs. Customers were getting confused; they didn't know who was copying whom.

Smith & Hawken made a couple of moves. We lowered prices even though a falling dollar was raising our costs. And we tripled the number of catalogs delivered. In the next two years we went from $2 million to $4 million to nearly $10 million in sales. By lowering prices, we had conveyed to the public that we were the most efficient and value-oriented company. The marketplace made the decision that Smith & Hawken was the leader in the field.

These decisions alone were not the cause of the turning point. If we hadn't been the first company in our niche, if we hadn't nailed down the best lines of merchandise, if we hadn't relentlessly pursued efficient processing and fulfillment systems internally, and if we had not been sufficiently financed, we would have been unable to make these moves. But after three or four years of hard work, it was a liberating feeling. We were in the middle of the market stream.

10

You Are the Customer, You Are the Company

Mrs. Green buys your widget and six months later returns it and wants her money back. New policy: "All goods must be returned within thirty days of purchase." Mr. Jones brings back your widget and says he bought it twenty days ago; he wants a refund. But you know that the discounter up the street just had a close-out sale on the item, and you suspect that Jones might have bought the widget cheaply there and now wants a full refund from you. New policy: "All items must be returned within thirty days and accompanied by the original receipt from this store." John Doe brings back one of your widgets and it looks as if it fell out of his car, or something equally serious. The widget is useless. New policy: "Damaged items will be exchanged only within thirty days of purchase, only if accompanied by original receipt from this store, and only if defect is a manufacturer's defect." Mrs. White orders a widget and asks you to ship it to her home upstate. Three weeks later it's returned to you in unrecognizable shape. The customer wants her money back but the trucker says she signed for it in "good condition" and he won't accept an insurance claim. New policy: "This merchandise left our store in first-class condition and shall not be returned for any reason without proper authorization. We definitely are not responsible for any damage whatsoever incurred at any time to any of our products while merchandise is in transit. Any merchandise returned to us will be refused. You must file a claim for damage, cost of repairs, shipping charges or replacement parts."

This last new policy is not a joke. That statement accompanied $17,000 worth of file cabinets delivered to our office. It was on a sticker glued to the front of every file cabinet. The cabinet maker had clearly had some prior problems with shipping damages, but I wonder about the wisdom of their solution. They could have worded their statement like this: "Before we shipped our cabinets to you, they were carefully inspected and confirmed to be in perfect condition. If they arrive in less than that condition something happened in transit. Give us a call. We are more than upset when anything comes between our craftsmanship and your satisfaction. We'll help you file your insurance claim against the common carrier. We'll make sure there is a follow-up with the carrier so this problem is expedited quickly and properly.

Thank you for choosing our cabinets. We are here to help."

We always hear that the customer comes first, the customer is always right, stay close to the customer. These credos are fine but a credo is not a business. The service provided by a company will not be guided by a sign posted on the wall. It will be guided by the views and ethics of the founders, owners, managers, and every last employee. The motto on the wall will have meaning only if it is truly the conviction of the person in charge. In the case of your business—you.

That's why so few North American companies have satisfactory customer relations. Management sees customers as an entity "outside" the company, and this is especially true in the case of the big corporations and retailers. Businesses are armed to the teeth to prevent fraud, abuse, hassles, and ripoffs coming from customers or suppliers. They have elaborate procedures for dealing with anything that might go wrong in the area of service. Meanwhile, and not coincidentally, just about everything has gone wrong with American business. No developed country in the world offers such miserable care and service to its customers.

A case in point. In February 1987, my wife and I purchased a new Dodge van. It was a fine car with one exception. It had an unusually strong and offensive odor emanating from the plastic. Everyone in our family who drove the car got headaches and experienced nausea, sometimes making us vomit. When we took it back to the service manager, he was sympathetic. He shampooed the whole car, and returned it. It still made us sick. We took it back a second time, to a new service manager. He drove it, shrugged it off as a "new car smell" and gave it back. We then left it outside for several weeks with all the doors and windows open. When we drove it again, it still gave us headaches. We took it back a third time. This time the service manager laughed at my wife. I called Chrysler. They said they would not see the car unless we got a notarized letter from our doctor saying that we had headaches. I refused, and wrote to Chrysler that I was going to return the car under the California "lemon law" code. They wrote back and said someone would get in touch. I waited seven weeks. I wrote again, and then they set up an appointment. When I got there, people who worked in the service department were pointing at me and sniggering. The Chrysler representative kept the car for the day and called the next day. When I returned the call, I was talking into a speaker phone. You could hear other people in the room but no one except the original representative identified himself. No doubt his boss was there, maybe a lawyer, who knows? His answer was it was simply a new car smell. Except for the first service manager, no one ever expressed concern. We were not believed, our experience was not accepted as valid, and our health or the possible effects on our health were never even mentioned or considered. As customers, we felt as if we were dealing with an organization that had been trained to avoid dealing with problems. From our point of view, the strategy of the dealer and Chrysler was to stonewall us, hoping that eventually the cause of the problem would dissipate. We will either "win" our arbitration case or sell the car. But in either case, everyone loses. We have lost time and money and Chrysler has lost a customer for life. But not just one customer. Two people who liked our van and were going to buy one have decided not to because of our experience. Our company will buy elsewhere.

But such attitudes are not confined to large corporations. Hanging above the counter of the delicatessen down the street from my office is that infamous sign of American commerce: WE RETAIN THE RIGHT TO REFUSE SERVICE TO ANYONE. Somewhere, tottering by now or dead in his grave, is the lawyer who invented that caveat. He should be proud because American business has retained not only that right, but also the right to refuse service to *every*one. Why think small?

But just as all the noise in the marketplace presents an opportunity for your own quiet, sensible message to penetrate, so all the bad service is a gift to you. The abandonment of the service ethic in America is the biggest single cause of our thriving small business culture. In many respects, service is the difference between the small business and the chain.

Carl Schmitt of University National Bank derides what he calls the "productization" of banking in this country in recent years. Schmitt and his employees substitute service for many of these products. And they were doing this for years before a survey by researchers at the University of Virginia business school showed that bank customers rank new products last on a list of improvements they would like to see. Better service ranked first. No one actually in the banking business should need a survey to know this.

A strong customer ethic must guide your business from the inception, even if it means losing money at times. As the business grows, you will have to take great care to preserve the quality of your service.

No matter whether you manufacture, grow, produce, distribute, or sell, you are "in service." The traditional business-page distinction between the "goods" and "services" sectors of the economy should not enter your thinking about your own business. Think of service as the final stage of production, which isn't completed until the customer is pleased. At Springfield Remanufacturing Center, employees responsible for major mistakes have been flown to distant cities to rectify the problems on the spot. They learn from the experience and share their insight with fellow workers, and the customer is impressed with a service he might not have expected.

At Smith & Hawken we sell products through our catalogs. Mail order cuts out the middleman, which is an advantage—one variable taken out of the equation. But this marketing method also creates a distance between us and our customers. They don't know us except through our service. We realized this quickly and decided that we must overcompensate for the apparent lack of convenience or control that a customer three thousand miles away might feel when ordering from us.

We have developed a set of guidelines that have helped us as we have grown—simple phrases that are at the heart of our company's "culture." We aren't a company of goals, standards, procedures, and exhortation. The rah-rah stuff is absent. Instead, we have concentrated on hiring people who embody the quality of service we strive for. It is difficult to teach someone to be helpful and serve others if he or she is misanthropic to begin with.

When we did get around to writing down our service guidelines we were surprised by them. They almost say more about our attitude toward ourselves than toward our customers. The customer comes first? Not really. The employee comes first. Employees' attitudes toward customers reflect their treatment by their employers. They cannot serve unless served. There's no way to instill a positive customer service ethic before you embody a positive employee ethic. Responsiveness in, responsiveness out.

Our goal as a company is to create customer service that is not just the best, but legendary.

Until recently, there was probably only one mail order company with "legendary" status when it comes to customer service, and that was L. L. Bean. Other companies do as well but they are either too young, too small, or too little known to merit the accolade. The point about "legendary" is that it presents a goal that is always moving ahead and will never be attained. It precludes complacency. It gives us all the psychic space we could ask for. "Legendary" gives everyone who deals with customers a rich sense of the possibilities. A customer called us once wanting to know how to deal with a wooden garden bench he had damaged during assembly. He lived a thousand miles from our office. We called a carpenter friend who lived near the customer and sent him over to fix the bench—no charge. Did that cost us money? Not in the long run.

You are the customer.

Companies can demand too much identification from their employees. A good customer service person must have

197

permission to say, without fear, "to heck with the company." This person must be able to do whatever is necessary to help an upset customer feel good about his or her relationship with the company. "Controlled, prudent, and expedient management" may sound fine in business school, but it usually means the customer feels screwed.

Several years ago, we came across one of our form letters that had been batted back and forth between "customer service" and our customer concerning an invalid American Express card. After investigating, we discovered that the error was ours. The customer was an old and dear one and her order had been held up for two months because of the crossed correspondence. A mail order nightmare come true: we had screwed our own customer. The person who discovered this sent her the order at no charge and we ate the $90 cost. From then on we stopped using first-class mail. Now, if there is a question or problem, we telephone. This call doesn't cost more money because it collapses the time between problem and solution, and eliminates paperwork. That particular episode reached my desk but it might not have. Our people have the authority—more than that, the responsibility—to say to heck with the company in favor of the customer.

When you are dealing with customer problems you have to discard the idea of profit. If you start to see a problem, a return, or an irate customer as red ink, you may avoid the best resolution to the problem.

The customer receives good service only when he or she perceives it as good service. Policies and procedures are helpful only as guides toward an end result. When the employee runs out of possibilities to make the customer happy, he or she must have the latitude to improvise to make it right. Most customer service employees operate in a state of fear that their own generosity with a customer will be viewed as foolishness by their boss. This situation will stifle flexible customer service.

Customers do not want a policy, they want a person. How many times have you been stopped short with the phrase, "I'm sorry, but that's company policy." Whatever policy you have about customer problems, be sure it's simple, open-ended, and based on trust. Most policies are based on mistrust. "Policy" has the same root word as "police."

You are the company.

Every person in the company carries the dignity and responsibility of ownership. Or should. I think the old-style companies owned by passive stockholders without employee ownership are dinosaurs. I don't believe companies will be able to thrive in the next decades without equitable and fair employee ownership plans. The pressure for this is coming from the smaller, entrepreneurial firms. We have an employee stock ownership plan at Smith & Hawken for a practical reason: we're too lazy to be bosses. We like the responsibility of management but aren't interested in the top-down control required of sole ownership.

If every employee is responsible as an owner, the payoff in customer relations is immediate. There will be no servile attitude in dealing the customers. Customers don't want that. They want responsible action, preferably from the first person they speak with. No one should have to go "higher up" to get permission to be considerate or even yielding.

There is no such thing as taking too much time with a customer because every customer is an exception.

Don't even try to measure service by some standard of productivity. You make a profit on your product, not on your people.

When production-line techniques came to retailing (dozens of checkout counters, long lines, anonymous clerks, self-service), we somehow saw this as growth and progress—modern times. In order for mass retailing to work, standardization of policy, systems, even floor layouts was deemed mandatory. Replication was the keystone of efficiency. The trade-off is obvious. In this brave new world, the customer has to adapt to the store policy rather than the store adapting to the customer's needs.

In the seventies, with its recession and subsequent inflation, competition among the mass merchandisers became fierce and resulted in staff cuts, hiring the lowest-cost employees (kids), and reducing the real wages paid. Improvements in efficiency were accomplished by labor-saving devices such as bar codes, which further reduced the human element in the transaction. The goal seemed to be an ideal world of commerce between machines. The customer might as well be a machine: there's nothing he or she can do about the procedures.

One proposition lies behind this drive toward dehumanized efficiency: a person adds very little value to a product once it has been built or produced. The best a person can do is plug in the cash register and get out of the way of the transaction. The system, as practiced by large retail and service businesses, denies individual needs and makes anyone who asks for special service seem odd or demanding. When the customer isn't an "exception," the business becomes unexceptional.

The boom in small businesses is a direct result of the misguidedness of this proposition. For the small business, the product has very little value without the person. Some larger businesses, too, defy the trend—Nordstrom on the West Coast, Federal Express, L. L. Bean, to name a few. But the list of exceptional companies of substantial size is so short it proves the rule.

Customers want a long-term relationship.

One of the great frustrations in commerce today is that our patronage and loyalty don't add up to anything. No matter how many years you shop at a chain store, nothing will ever change in your relationship with that store or with those people (you will have lasted a lot longer than the employees, anyway). That sameness of experience is the whole idea behind the store. McDonald's does not and cannot care how many times you have bought a Big Mac. Of course the franchise wants you to return tomorrow for another dose, but if you don't, someone else will. But we as human beings don't feel, act, and comprehend with such uniformity. We would like our activities, even such mundane ones as shopping for food, to add up, to build a relationship, to establish trust.

At the moment of transaction, the customer is vulnerable—to you and your action, to the respect you grant or withhold. The one promise held out by money is that some sort of satisfaction will result from this purchase. The customer wants to buy respectful treatment. I don't look upon granting this respect as a business ethic, I consider it an expression of sympathy. As a businessperson, you have an opportunity to confound the world's cynicism, to put a dent in the accumulated deceits that have preceded this transaction. Or you can add to the load.

I live in a small town. I have a personal account down the street at the Bank of America, and I run an annual payroll through the same branch that totals about $2 million. But when my wife cashes a check, the clerk calls up the outstanding balance on her computer terminal before cashing it. The manager and assistant manager of the bank are wonderful people. I know them. But they are in an organization that voids their good human qualities. Their tellers are underpaid, turn over quickly so they can't get to know the customers, and even if they did know us, they are stuck with work rules that may make sense in a big-city, downtown branch but are onerous in my small town.

Across the street from the bank is a food market that behaves quite the opposite. I can cash a check anytime without a purchase. No one has ever asked for an I.D. even for my first check. If I'm without my wallet, I can pay later. This store has sales per square foot many times higher than the national average. Their customers are fiercely loyal.

If it doesn't feel right, make it right.

You must give permission to your employees to do what they think is right. Give them responsibility. A salesperson at Nordstrom left the store to drive a client to the airport to catch a flight. No policy book could cover all such contingencies. Don't even try to concoct one. Our policy book says this: it has to feel right. Feeling right counts for everything because when the product and the money are exchanged, a feeling, sweet or sour, is what we're left with.

Of course, this "policy" requires you to trust your employees. If you don't, it stands to reason that you'll try to protect yourself with strict procedures. But these don't protect a business, they isolate it.

A job isn't done until it's checked.

If our work is 99 percent error free, we can theoretically reduce that 1 percent error rate to less than one-tenth of 1 percent if we do the work twice. That sounds like an expensive and rather small reduction, but I don't think it is. Smith & Hawken processes one to two thousand orders a day. We are too bombarded by the complexity of our work to expect error-free results. If we don't build in redundancies, the customer will do our error-checking for us and will not be so forgiving.

Do it once and do it yourself.

This sounds like a contradiction of the previous guideline, but it's not. An example will explain. A customer calls and says, "I did not receive my pencil with my flower markers." She should have. Our person answering the phone can take this information, walk to the warehouse, grab the pencil, put it in an envelope, and address the envelope. Whenever possible, and it usually is possible, one person follows through on the entire customer service situation. We do not create layers of hirelings who shuffle instructions back and forth among themselves. We have a lateral organization in which each person uses a broad scope of skills and fulfills

203

a range of jobs. We eliminate delegation and encourage integration. This doesn't always make for "efficiency," but it makes the work more interesting.

When in doubt, ask. When not in doubt, ask.
This sounds like a contradiction of the last guideline, but it merely means that if our person isn't exactly sure what's required, we're not going to bluff our way through. We get a bewildering array of questions from our customers. We aim to answer every one, and it's okay not to know at first. The notion of asking when not in doubt is more subtle. We are a learning-based company, and a spirit of inquiry is intrinsic to that goal. People don't want hierarchical organizations. They want to work in an atmosphere of cooperation. This doesn't happen when someone poses as the world's greatest expert, appearing to possess or actually possessing vital information that is shared only when convenient.

If you are not in doubt, you may be kidding yourself.

A mistake is not a mistake. It is a chance to improve the company.
Opportunity arises from flux, uncertainty, even confusion. You should keep this in mind when developing your business and even afterward, when it's a growing concern. A mistake is usually where the predicted didn't happen. The unpredicted is the gap between perception and reality. The unpredicted is your best toehold on reality because it is from these events that don't "go right" that you can discover what is really happening with your business. Most businesses crow about what's going right and look on what doesn't as aberration. Most business books do the same

thing as they idolize the wildly successful. But in your business, the mistakes, your own or others', will lead you most directly to better products, cost savings, new ideas, and better customer service. How long did Ford ignore the exploding gas tanks in the Pinto? Or A. H. Robins the Dalkon Shield? For that matter, how long will IBM ignore the fact that their computer keyboards are slow, cumbersome, and a decided disadvantage for the serious word processor?

We were making a "normal" error rate in our shipping department: 1 percent of mis-ships or short-ships. That might sound high, but it's standard for the industry. Normal but unacceptable. In order to change it we reinvented the cookie jar. Our mistakes led us to a new way of doing things.

We figured out that every shipping mistake cost us $10 to straighten out, and unknown sums in indirect costs such as subsequent lost business. One percent of $10 is ten cents. That's the amount we put into the cookie jar for every order filled. For every mistake we took out $10. If we improved on our 1 percent error rate, we'd have money left over, which was divided up among the packers. Packers don't stay for long periods. That's a high-turnover job, so not many of them participate in our profit-sharing plan. We needed a substitute for the short-term packers and the cookie jar worked. The packers would benefit from any improvements they made. The error rate dropped almost immediately to two-tenths of 1 percent, an 80 percent reduction.

We still have a long way to go.

One final point about service, and a vitally important

one it is. There can be no good service without a good product. Our return policy is simple: if you are dissatisfied at any time for any reason, or no reason at all, you may return any Smith & Hawken product for a full refund or replacement. The most frugal thing we can do is be certain our products are of the highest quality. If it should cost us so much to replace products that we have to go out of business, then we should go out of business. A no-holds-barred return policy is the litmus test for quality. The restrictive return policies and parsimonious attitudes of many companies stem from a deeper reality. Their goods are not so good.

What about the customers? What are their duties and obligations? A good company needs good, alert customers who will talk, write, criticize, and praise. The economy is the most democratic institution in the world and it, too, fails without voter participation. Your business will fail without good customer feedback. It behooves you to change places with the customer, to think about the kind of customer you want, then to return to work with the intention of creating a business that will attract this customer.

Here are a few suggestions on how to be a good customer:

1. *Complain.* If you don't, who will? It takes only a minute, you will feel better, and the company will benefit.
2. *Praise.* This is just as important as criticism. It spurs the business to reward creative and constructive work.

206

3. *Be articulate.* You know what you want, the company may not. Be as specific as you can about what you want and spell it out, simply and clearly.

4. *Demand quick service.* There is no excuse for slow service today. Technology allows any company to process orders or problems within twenty-four hours. Don't believe otherwise.

5. *Be quick yourself.* If something is wrong, pounce. Don't wait four months. After a delay, the company will have a harder time believing you.

6. *Be kind.* When you reach the company, assume that the voice on the other end is a human being like yourself. Let him or her have the pleasure of helping you. If that doesn't work . . .

7. *Be persistent.* If necessary, go upstairs. Then go higher. In many companies, the top has no idea what mayhem transpires down below.

I once wrote a magazine piece about customer service, and a shorter accompanying piece about being a good customer. The first piece became a popular reprint request. That was encouraging, but I was more interested in the lack of response to the much shorter piece—not a single reprint request. Those companies must have missed my point: there is no good service without good, sometimes painful, feedback and criticism to engender it.

11

In Good Company

W HEN I worked on a farm, we managed herds. We managed rangeland. Friends managed feedlots. So I am amused but dismayed when someone talks about managing people. You don't ever manage people—you *work with* them. For your business to succeed, you must take exceedingly good care of your people. This is not a chore or a responsibility, it is the most rewarding aspect of being in business, yet it is the area in which most business-es, large and small, fail.

If people are honest about it, you will find that the majority of them are not satisfied with their jobs, their work, or their relationship with "management." One of the strongest reasons so many people want to go into business for themselves is not the allure of business, but a desire to get away from their current stifling jobs. It is well within your power as a businessperson to create an atmosphere that is not stifling.

Even the most benighted corporations are aware of this disenchantment and yearning for independence of their employees, but their efforts to counter it with new programs within the bureaucracy are wrongheaded at best, self-destructive at worst. Popular now among large corporations are ambitious "organizational development" programs designed to remake the corporate culture by something close to indoctrination. An example is Pacific Bell, one of the Baby Bells spun off from AT&T. PacBell is spending an estimated $60 million per year on what one employee called a "dress code for the mind." Thousands of employees are placed into two-day seminars at regular intervals, where they learn about end-state vision (goals), path forwards (plans), and alignment (agreement), all packaged under the rubric of Leadership Development. (It is safe to say that in the history of the world no true leader has emerged from a seminar, and I suppose it is equally true that no seminar ever emerged from a leader.)

The employees learn about value modes of behavior, how as individuals and teams they can "seek and use freedom to improve performance toward increasing standards of excellence" so that they might "earn more space to contribute."

Compare this corporate philosophy with the one at Esprit de Corp., the $800 million clothing company started by Doug and Susie Tompkins. At Esprit, employees are given free language, kayaking, and aerobics classes. Lunch is subsidized. One-half of the price of any ticket to a cultural event is paid by the company. At Esprit, a highly creative environment is cultivated and encouraged. There is no need to require people to listen to such statements as this at PacBell: "Creativity is a key asset and individuals and teams will want to and will achieve ever-increasing levels of performance consistent with ever-increasing standards as they seek freedom and are enabled to be creative within the context of our clearly understood and accepted business purpose."

Is someone being paid by the word?

The irony is that the program stemmed out of PacBell's divestiture from AT&T in 1984, and the company's desire to move from a "compliance culture," which was okay in the days of regulation, to a more open corporate culture that could be more responsive to the new era of deregulation. This goal is fine, but instituting programs such as PacBell's is changing without change. "Management training" is "organizational development" is "leadership enhancement" is . . . birds of a feather.

People want to be, and must be, treated as people. PacBell-type programs send another message with their jargon that is nothing more than a new multisyllabic bureaucratese. As a businessperson, you teach by example, and lead the same way. When a large business organization goes flat because of the accumulated baggage of bad decisions, it cannot consult its way out of the problem. It cannot hire its way out, either. Money cannot purchase creativity, but it can certainly stifle it. PacBell justified its expenditures for "retraining" on the basis that even as little as a 2 or 3 percent increase in productivity at the $7.6 billion giant would add considerably to the bottom line.

But what if PacBell had followed the path of the smaller Springfield Remanufacturing Center of Springfield, Missouri, and sat down with the employees to ask the simple but compelling question, "What kind of company do we want to live and work in?" Or, better yet, what if the West Coast utility had asked the employees, rather than consultants, to make PacBell a better company?

Your new business won't be tempted to spend $60 million on leadership development, and your small size to some extent buffers you from even the temptation to deal with your people as bureaucrats and functionaries. The closer anyone is to really working with people, as opposed to passing along orders and paperwork to unseen faces, the lower the impulse to standardize the relationship. Bureaucracies are usually big, but not always. I've seen businesses with seven employees run like the post office.

In 1985 the Newhouse newspaper chain purchased *The New Yorker* magazine. Less than two years later the new owner dismissed William Shawn, its venerable, even legendary editor, without consulting the staff or writers. In the magazine's sixty-two-year history it had had only two editors, founder Harold Ross and Shawn. After paying $146 million for the magazine, Newhouse no doubt wanted to get its money's worth. But in the process of removing Shawn with no notice or grace, it destroyed decades of valuable goodwill created by the previous owners. Some of the best writers quit. The Newhouse saga is repeated again and again in American business, and it is here that businesses most consistently embarrass and hurt themselves. The firing of an employee has its roots in the medieval practice of ostracism. If a village in Europe or China wanted to censure and remove a member of its society, the townspeople went to the offender's home and burned it to the ground, along with all the possessions inside. That's how they fired someone. It's unfortunate but apt that this term "firing" lives on to describe the way we "terminate" employment.

Firing is failure. Everybody is at fault. That's the simplest way to look at it. The best way to avoid firing people is to hire well in the first place. Hiring is one of the most critical activities of any business, and you should learn to do it well. It can make an enormous difference in your success. I estimate that one-half of all business problems originate with the perceptions, attitudes, and practices of the owner. The other half of the problems are caused by faulty hiring. The real estate adage applies: you make money when you buy a building, not when you sell it.

Hiring is an art. Recent laws and court rulings that give employees more rights in relationship to the employer were needed and deserved. They do, however, make the relationship between employer and prospective or current employee more delicate and complex, and they make hiring well even more important. Except under special circumstances, you may no longer ask questions about a person's age, marital status, birthplace, arrest record, or children. You may not even discharge or refuse to hire a person if he has falsely denied prior arrests. This is now federal law. In the case of terminating an employee, recent court settlements make your company extremely susceptible to lawsuits for what might appear to the employer as a justified reason for dismissal. For example, you may not fire an employee for a heinous act if the method of termination does not conform precisely to the employee manual. Most companies have reacted to these rulings and laws with guidelines that make the hiring process controlled, predictable, and deadly dull. The fact is that the qualities you are looking for in a human being have nothing to do with all those unaskable questions. Discrimination is useless, but discernment is a must.

If you hire well from the beginning, you will have people who won't need to have their thinking "seminared," and you certainly won't have to fire them. Here are some ideas to keep in mind as you seek good people to work with.

HIRE THE PERSON, NOT THE POSITION

At Smith & Hawken, the quality we are most concerned with is the person's "heart." Is he a good person? Does he like people and want to work with them, in the office, and assist them, as customers? Does his work express these qualities?

We're more interested in what kind of person a potential employee is than in where the person worked before or what he or she has or hasn't accomplished. It's a comment on our times that "successful" people are seen as those who get their way, overcome opposition, and achieve their goals regardless of others. Lee Iacocca may have saved Chrysler, but a person with his ego and sense of self-importance would be unemployable in the successful companies I know. If every person you hire is bristling with self-confidence and a purposeful sense of overachievement, you will have your hands full sorting out the egos. Between the extremes of aggressive egoists and passive yes-men are people who have the qualities that allow them to work with others. The key term here is *with*, because the successful company is not the sum of individual actions, but of individual interactions.

When hiring at Smith & Hawken, we will often look for people who have not thrived in the conventional business world. There would probably be a good reason for their "failure" to fit in at, for example, Pacific Bell. Not being able to adjust to a hierarchical organization means that a person didn't get into the habit of self-denial for the sake of employment. They are the changelings of the world of commerce, people who couldn't find a job or a company that allowed them to be as expressive of their humanity and their selves as they needed to be. These commercial changelings abound in this world. They are ordinary people of great sensitivity and perception, qualities too often ignored in the business world. These people make wondrous employees, even if they seem quiet or self-effacing. Given the proper environment they are veritable late-bloomers who will surprise even themselves with their loyalty, high spirits, and productivity.

The head of our distribution center is a former woodworker who had been a fireman before that. He walked in off the street, made some shelves and toolracks for us, and asked for a job. He now supervises fifty people and manages two acres of warehouse—packing, quality control, and shipping. He had no prior experience in any of these areas. I estimate that 90 percent of the people who work with me are doing something completely different from their previous job experience. There are no experts, but there are a lot of good intentions, tolerance for error, and support for learning.

HIRE PEOPLE YOU
LOOK UP TO

You must never hire anyone you look down on or think less of than yourself. Your employees will know how you feel about them anyway, because we all know how others think of us, whether we deny it or finesse it.

Your employees will be an accurate reflection of who you are. After all, you, or the people you hired, hired the employees and established their working environment. If you are the founder, manager, or head of your company, whom do you want to work with? It seems self-defeating to hire someone you believe you can take advantage of or exploit. Although many of us have faulty self-esteem, it must take *enormously* low self-esteem to want to surround yourself with people you think are inferior. But it happens all the time in small businesses: people in the workplace are treated in a condescending manner. Your chances of sainthood will not increase when you choose the world of commerce. Precisely because you and I are ordinary people with flaws as well as virtues, we must assiduously maintain respect for all associates.

If you start or run a business, you will spend most of your waking life there. Why not create a society you want to live in? The intangible bonds and connections among human beings are not measurable or even very analyzable, but they pervade the heart and fiber of every business. The people you work with are your most immediate society: their qualities, consciousness, and values comprise your environment. If you would like to improve the society around you, it makes no sense whatsoever to hire any but the best people you can possibly find. Your employees shouldn't admire you. That is kid stuff. You should admire your employees.

DON'T USE PERSONNEL MANAGERS OR HEADHUNTERS

Hiring and being hired has become a highly institutionalized, "professionalized" process. Big companies employ personnel managers who read trade magazines, go to seminars and workshops, and have national conventions— all on the subject of hiring a human being.

The hirelings, in turn, hire résumé services and counselors who conduct mock interviews on video and dispense advice on dressing for that awful moment of absurdity, the job interview. The whole business of hiring people and finding jobs has become perverted beyond recognition. In order to restore some semblance of reality to the process, see each person interviewing for the job as if he were your best customer, instead of a supplicant. Don't put people through the sterile process of going through "personnel." Get them immersed in the company. Let the interviewing process be conducted by different people in the company. Invite the interviewees to a company softball game, or even to a meeting. Make them feel at home. Ask them to criticize the company instead of allowing them to offer up fawning praise.

In a larger business, use personnel managers to assist you in finding people, to be sure, but leave the actual hiring to those who will work with the new person. Personnel department functions should be limited to support, assistance, morale boosting, listening, arranging softball games and parties, and playing April Fools' jokes.

The best source of new employees is a satisfied worker. Create a business that is the cat's pajamas to work in, and you will be deluged with the friends, associates, and relatives of employees who would like to work with you. They will be your best recruits.

While it's possible to hire employees' friends, you have to be careful when hiring your own friends. The hiring of a new person should be the beginning of a relationship: clean, straightforward, and without preconception. The friend might feel he is in a privileged position in the company, and that would be bad. Or he might go overboard in the opposite direction and refrain from constructive criticism, say, because of a fear that it would harm the old friendship. That would be bad, too. The job is a new world for the employee and the less baggage from the past he brings to it, the better.

Hiring a friend might help the friendship, or hurt it, or even ruin it. The main question is, How would it help or hurt the business? Don't let emotional considerations interfere with clear-headed hiring.

Do the hiring any way you want to, but make it real, do

it yourself, and be sure not to break the law. Do not institutionalize the process so thoroughly that you lose the key to your whole enterprise: the rich and diverse interaction of human beings, committed to working together. The law is there to protect the individual, but I do not think its intent is to impose a dispiriting orthodoxy on the process.

CREATE HYBRID VIGOR

When different strains of plants or animals are cross-bred, "hybrid vigor" is sometimes the result. The best traits of each species combine in a new species that is superior to either parent. Plant and animal breeders are always seeking hybrid vigor. The smart employer does the same thing.

At Smith & Hawken, we often hire someone who has done a good job in one area at another company, and place this person into an entirely different set of circumstances within ours. At first blush this might seem to be handicapping ourselves, especially if the new position requires skills and expertise that would be a problem for the new employee during a transition period. But it doesn't turn out this way. If the person is generally competent (as indicated by good performance in the other job), and if the new job is suited to his or her abilities, he or she will be on a very steep learning curve. The individual will see the work with new eyes and spot the conventional wisdoms that are wrong. He or she will absorb enormous amounts of new information, gladly accepting advice and support. This person will not be afraid to admit not knowing something because you don't expect anyone to know everything. You expect the person to learn.

Such employees will not conform, but transform. Their naiveté will often lead them to new ideas and ways of doing things a pro would have overlooked. This is hybrid vigor in employees.

Kris McDivitt is the general manager of Lost Arrow, the parent corporation of Patagonia and the other Yvon Chouinard companies. The woman Chouinard describes as his "bombproof belay" (a mountaineering term that refers to rope holding fast and means the strongest support in the world) began work for him in 1972 as an assistant packer in the shipping department. She has since held almost every job in the company with the exception of blacksmith and rurp grinder.

The head of data processing at Smith & Hawken is an ex-seminarian who had never held a job in his life, and who had never touched a computer before coming to work. He was, however, an outstanding pianist and composer, and my thought was that he would take to software and programming with the same genius that inspired his music. He did.

A friend of mine was a schoolteacher when I last saw her years ago. At a chance meeting more recently, she told me she was organizing national conferences involving hundreds of CEOs from major corporations. I inquired how that was working out. She laughed and said handling those guys was a piece of cake compared to handling preschoolers. Whoever hired her for that job understood hybrid vigor.

The opposite of hybrid vigor is inbreeding, and the inbreeding of the knower with the known is dangerous in business, too. Someone hired for a position he's supposed to understand thoroughly will feel reluctant to admit it when he doesn't know everything about the new job—yet how can he know everything, because every company operates differently. The newly hired "expert" will feel that his pride is on the line with every decision. You've hired a senior market analyst, so he'd better analyze the market in a senior sort of way. How comfortable would he feel coming to you and reporting the truth, that the market has him stumped?

Consider your own situation as the owner of a small business. You didn't know everything, or even a lot, about that business when you started it, but that didn't worry you. You understood your own abilities and, more important, your adaptabilities. You have been practicing hybrid vigor from the very beginning. Keep it at the heart of your business as you hire people and grow.

After hiring a good employee, you have to keep her. It does no good to find the right person but then treat her in such a way that she's looking for another job within six months. The best way to keep good people is to create an atmosphere of hybrid vigor throughout your business, from top to bottom. Keep people active in as many aspects of your operations as possible. Give them as many different responsibilities as possible. Responsibility is participation, and this sense of participation in the "big picture" of the business is the key factor that will keep your employees growing as people and as productive employees.

Japanese companies do not allow a person to stay in the same position for too many years, particularly if he or she is good. The person is moved around in the organization, mixing up responsibilities. This is a valuable employee, who will know how the different parts of a company are connected. At Smith & Hawken, we cross-train all permanent staff. Everyone is at least taught to use the computer, take phone orders on-line, and answer customer service requests. If the individual stays, we add to the list.

DON'T GROW FASTER THAN
YOUR EMPLOYEES CAN

There are two main obstacles to rapid business growth. One can be economic, usually a shortage of capital funds. The second is often overlooked. Businesses that grow too fast or in the wrong way overwhelm the adaptive capacity of the people who work there. When this happens, people go on "overload" and slowly withdraw, perhaps without being aware of it, so that they can maintain their personal equilibrium. Just as your business can outstrip your ability to raise capital, you can outstrip your employees' ability to learn and develop.

To avoid this, approach your people in a way that rarely happens in American business. Sit down with them and explain how you think the business is going to grow in the next year, and how you believe this will affect the different jobs or departments. Then find out what each of the employees thinks about the scenario. Find out how they feel this growth will affect their jobs. Find out whether they think the operation can handle the rapid hiring and training of new people. In short, find out whether your people will be with you or against you. They'll appreciate the invitation to participate in the planning stage rather than being in the positions of employees of most companies who hear about what's happening after the fact.

Alice Medrich of Cocolat learned this lesson the hard way. Her cake and pastry business in Berkeley, California, grew rapidly in the early 1980s, and cash flow problems forced her to delay what had been regular pay raises. But she didn't inform the employees about the reason for the delay. They organized a union, went on strike for a week, and many of them, friends of hers, eventually left the company. Moral: Be in charge and let everyone know what's going on and why.

Furthermore, employees are often closer than owners to the problems engendered by rapid growth. They see and feel the strain and weak points, and they can identify these areas of vulnerability. This is critical if a business is growing extremely fast. The potential problems in rapid business expansion remind me of the growth metaphor described by Paul Ehrlich in *The Population Bomb*. Ehrlich postulates a lake in which there is rapid plant growth due to too much nitrogen running off from the fields. Every twenty-four hours the water hyacinth mass doubles in size. If the plant continues to grow at that rate, the lake will be totally clogged on the thirtieth day, and it will die. But just one day before that, it will be 50 percent open.

When a company grows exponentially, it can become the lake on the twenty-ninth day. The problems may not appear to be critical until it's too late. The exhilaration of growth can occlude the problems of morale, planning, production, and marketing created by it.

I have seen more suffering in business caused by too-rapid growth than by any other cause. It creates unusual stress, distorts judgment, precipitates financial crises even as the money is pouring in. It can tear a company apart, as it did Apple Computer. Stay close to your employees, be sure they understand the nature and rate of growth, and then listen to them.

5–15 REPORTS

These were invented by Yvon Chouinard of Patagonia. A 5–15 report is so named because it requires no more than fifteen minutes to write or five minutes to read. Handwritten or typed, it is submitted every Friday by most employees of the company.

The first part of the report is a simple description of what a person did during the week. The employees find that, when they describe their work week after week, their ability to really describe what's going on becomes refined and more detailed. And if they do not become more adept at defining their work, if their reports become boring and repetitive, that comes through as a danger signal: employee requires a transfusion, or job needs to be more challenging, or both.

The second part of the 5–15 reports is a blunt description of the employees' morale, and the morale they see in their department.

The last part requires everyone to present one idea that will improve his or her job, department, or the company—one idea a week, fifty-two ideas a year.

Chouinard's idea for the 5–15 report was picked up by Doug Tompkins of Esprit. Both men travel extensively, spending as much as six months of the year away from their company headquarters, and the 5–15 is a way for them to keep in touch. (Doug calls it his M.B.A. style: Managing by Being Away.) Regardless of where they are, Chouinard and Tompkins receive their 5–15s every week.

The owners receive the reports of the department heads, who in turn have received the reports from their associates. No one has more than two dozen to read, so there's no overburden on time or attention. Department heads sometimes trade reports. The 5–15s are a direct, efficient, and consistent source of communication that knits together the parts of the company.

We have 5–15s at Smith & Hawken, too, and the unspoken rule is that all ideas, suggestions, and problems presented in the reports are acted upon within one week. A longer delay would be ineffective and demoralizing.

Here is one 5–15 report submitted by our head buyer at Smith & Hawken:

> This week I continued to work on the fall catalog. I'm putting together product details for Allen and have given him vendor information. Bill and I met and did some projecting of new foreign items. . . . I placed foreign orders which we projected. I reviewed catalog changes with Alice and assigned [the] individual pages.
>
> Although I reviewed purchasing with Allen, I'm very frustrated in this area—can't believe we backordered a product as easy to get as FloraLife.
>
> I was told the hammocks from Mexico that were lost couldn't be traced by USPS. I made a few calls and

initiated a tracer and found them in a storeroom in Oakland. I feel bad about this. However, I think there may be another way to ship and am in the process of finding out.

Morale is good (it's amazing how quickly I forget pain and labor). I love my new desk. It sheds a new light on everything and I guess good vibes are left over from Lewis. You can't believe how much better it is sitting here.

My idea this week is to replace the present word-processor with a new one. No one likes to use the present system. Cumbersome, and the printer is noisy. How about some Macs?

GO FOR BROKES

Convinced of the usefulness of the 5–15s, Smith & Hawken invented the Go for Broke. This is an annual affair every September, our slowest month, although some departments do them midyear as well. The 5–15s are suspended for the month to make way for the Go for Brokes.

The Go for Broke report is an attempt by *every person* in the company to list everything in his or her department, or anywhere else at Smith & Hawken, that he or she believes is broken and needs fixing—including relationships between employees. It is a company-wide inventory of what needs to be noticed, changed, improved, or checked. The writers of the longest, most original, most humorous, and best thought out Go for Brokes get awards such as all-expense-paid weekends at a country inn. It took us five months to dig out from under the voluminous response to the first Go for Brokes, a detailed examination of every last crevice of the company. In most cases, the things needing repair were fixed by the person identifying the problem.

We have had three Go for Brokes, and I have not seen or heard about anything that improved a company so thoroughly as these have. Within the five-month period following the submission of the first reports, we made over one thousand changes in response to them.

TITMOUSES AND ROBINS

Professor Allan C. Wilson, an ornithologist, noted that when British milk companies changed to aluminum seals on the milk bottle, it didn't take long for titmouses to discover the ease with which they could poke their beaks through and get at the cream. From the Scottish highlands to Cornwall, titmouses found a new source of food. Robins, however, as a group have still not figured out how to pierce the seals. They may never. Robins are highly territorial and spend much of their time establishing and protecting their territories from transgression by other robins, while titmouses move in flocks and do not have territories, and spend more time in communication. They learn faster.

Your small business does not want to be a robin organization. But this is what usually happens in mature companies, and for two reasons.

One is staffing. Most companies are overstaffed, with too many people to go around for the work available. The people, quietly but surely, sense their redundancy. When people know they are not being fully utilized, their natural reaction is to protect the work they do have. They establish territories just like the robins. One of the ways they do this is to politicize information—share it unequally. If you work in an organization that develops this territorial sense of status and title, then you may not be rewarded if you give certain information to certain people. Most likely, you won't give it to the people under you.

The slightly understaffed company avoids this danger because people need each other more. With "too much" work to do, people are quite willing to share that work and the responsibility and information that go with it. They are grateful for help, and they don't perceive those who help them as threatening, because these people have all they can handle, too. People would rather be overutilized than underworked. One is challenge, the other boredom. Of course you have to watch out for overwork, leading to burnout, but if the small businessperson stays in close touch with the operation, he'll strike the right balance almost automatically.

The second reason businesses degenerate into robin organizations is that the employees often imitate the boss. People aim to please, and employees constantly observe the owner for cues as to what constitutes appropriate behavior. The owner or founder of a company sets the tone for attitude and behavior. If this individual is open, sharing, and attentive to what other people in the company say, then he or she will see this open behavior in employees. This openness is crucial. Information has to flow laterally in a company in order for it to work as a learning tool. To achieve this lateral flow, people have to work in teams and the owner has to get down to where the action is.

If the owner is aloof and does not share information, then

he or she can be sure others will follow suit. Information does not flow easily across antagonistic barriers. An owner who sets employee against employee and production unit against production unit is kidding himself. You can certainly get people to work out of the fear and anxiety fostered by this competition, but in doing so you will stymie the most important growing quality your company must have—everyone's ability to learn and share. In an atmosphere of politicized information, there will be less information and it will flow either into little cul-de-sacs or upward. People will work for their superiors, not for their company.

I am not arguing for an organization without leaders. A boss is needed where control is necessary. This is sometimes required in any situation. But an organization as a whole does *not* require control. Instead, it requires astute attention to detail, liberal and honest communication, and the mutual trust of workers and colleagues in order for them to act on behalf of the whole company while dealing with their specific jobs.

The Verger

O NE OF the difficulties of writing this book was the necessity of avoiding any implication that you should fashion your business after mine or after any of the others described. Nothing could be further from my purpose. For that reason, I have deliberately kept the descriptions and profiles of the different businesses quite short. I include stories to draw a parallel or make a point, never to serve as models. The only model you should keep in mind is one of integrity, your own and your company's, in all relations with suppliers, customers, and community. The world wants to support the best you can be simply because it has seen too much of the worst that we can be.

Growing a Business

I end the book with a story, not mine, but one by W. Somerset Maugham. "The Verger" expresses easily and touchingly the elemental characteristics that are the heart of a successful business. A verger is a functionary in the lower range of the Church of England hierarchy. The verger's name in the story is Albert Edward Foreman, cockney, a man of tact, firmness, self-assurance, and unimpeachable character. His opportunity arises from a problem, his business from a self-expressed need. He succeeds because of guilelessness, not cunning. His business grows out of his patient observation, not his avarice. His satisfaction derives from the process, not from a monetary goal. In short, the verger never veers or compromises in order to grow his business.

As the story begins, Albert has been the verger in a London church for sixteen years. Prior to that he was "in service."

Immediately following a christening one day, the new vicar of the church summons Albert, acknowledges his excellent service to the church, but then confesses, "A most extraordinary circumstance came to my knowledge the other day and I felt it my duty to impart it to the churchwardens. I discovered to my astonishment that you could neither read nor write."

The verger agrees that this is the case. Offered three months in which to learn to read and write, he declines the offer, feeling that he is too old a dog to learn new tricks. To his astonishment, he is therefore dismissed from his post. A verger is ordinarily hired for life.

As Albert walks home jobless, he makes a wrong turn and, at the same time, desires a cigarette, a rare treat he indulges when tired. Gold Flake cigarettes are his brand. But as he walks down the long street of shops, he cannot find one that sells cigarettes. Reaching the end of the block—and blocks in London can be very long—he turns around and walks it again to be sure. No smokes.

The next day he locates a small shop to let and, with the money he had saved from his years as a verger, he becomes a tobacconist and news agent within the month. He sells a few sweets as well. His wife believes this is a terrible comedown, but Albert points out that times have changed and the church isn't what it was. And his shop does well. A year later he finds another long street lacking a tobacconist and he opens a second shop and employs a manager. These two stores do so well he begins walking all over London. When he finds a long street without a tobacco shop and an empty store to let, he takes it. After ten years Albert has ten shops.

One morning he enters his bank to deposit the takings for the week, and the bank manager asks to speak with him. The manager comments that the stores have amassed a considerable amount of capital, and he suggests that there might be better ways to invest it and gain a better rate of return. The bank manager will be glad to arrange everything if Albert will fill out a transfer form.

"Well, sir, that's just it. I can't. I know it sounds funny-like, but there it is, I can't read or write, only me name, an' I only learnt to do that when I went into business."

The bank manager is aghast. "And do you mean to say that you've built up this important business and amassed a fortune . . . without being able to read or write? Good

233

God, man, what would you be now if you had been able
to?"

"I can tell you that," said Mr. Foreman, a little smile on
his aristocratic features. "I'd be verger of St. Peter's,
Neville Square."

Acknowledgments

There would be fewer books by this author if it were not for Stewart Brand, the former editor and still publisher of the *Whole Earth Review*. As with my last book, *The Next Economy*, it was Stewart's nudges that prompted the antecedents to the book, articles which he gamely published despite my protestations. It was because there was such a warm reader response that the book took flight. While writing this, I lost contact with Stewart for the best of reasons: he was embroiled in his own book, *The Media Lab, Inventing the Future at MIT* (Viking). It's a marvelous book and I'm glad to have him back to invent my future.

Since I have the only literary agent in New York who

answers his phone after midnight, I will embarrass Joe Spieler further by saying he does his best work then, and did so for me, offering counsel, jokes (some bad), comments on the Mets game, and editorial encouragement on demand. This extraordinary act will no doubt unlist his phone, but it was great while it lasted. In the Manhattan phone book, check under "Deke."

Nora Gallagher, a writer of more note than I, took time from other deadlines to give the book its initial shape and form. This was all agreed to over a steaming plate of hot rice noodles and Singha beer, a meal she may have regretted later. Thai food has been known to cause such lapses of judgment. Her willingness to subordinate her deadlines to my own was an act of grace of greater proportion than she could possibly realize.

Diane McQuarie, a writer about women's business, came to my office once to consult about her newsletter and ended up as a research assistant and tireless contributor. May that serve as a warning to all others who seek consultation from authors. Not only did Diane serve the book with the greatest of enthusiasm, but she went on to work on the TV program at KQED, a further gift to us all.

Marjorie Poore and Joanne Locktov masterminded the PBS series, not only finding people, budgets, and a sponsor, but working diligently to ensure the series' success on every level. Marjorie proved herself to be a consummate organizer, a behind-the-scenes impresario managing the impossible task of having a book, TV program, and ancillary promotions conceived, created, and completed within one year. There should be awards for her breed.

To the Marketing Council at ComputerLand, especially

Marian Murphy and Ron Kuhl, a special thanks for the good cheer, unflagging support and faith in a project that most corporations would have put to a slow bureaucratic death. Coming as it did in the midst of their change in ownership, it was even more remarkable.

For Anna, my wife, who for the fourth time became a widow to a manuscript, I have nothing but awe for the understanding and sweetness shown during those difficult periods of pressure and absence. I have yet to meet a secure writer, and she, sensing the fragility of my moods, ushered in every day with hope and light.

In the final months of the book, Mike and Patty Bryan camped in my studio with their Macintosh and editorial skills. Calmly, with gentility born of their southern extraction, they graciously formed, reformed and constructed the previous months' outpourings into the form the book has today. It would have taken me a year to do what they did in a month, but longer still to do it with such humor and panache. Without their effort, the book would simply not exist today. It was a combination of efforts so fortuitous that Michael and I have set forth upon the next book, this time as coauthors.

To Bo, George, Elaine, Elyse, and the others at *Inc.* magazine, thank you for including portions of this book in the only business publication that does not separate human values from economic values. It is an association I will honor.

The following people, although not directly involved with the book, have supported this work with their big hearts, bright eyes, and inspired lives: Corrine, Marty, Alec and Marilyn, Bruce and the entire camera crew; Linda, two

Alices, Mercedes, Dave, Bill, Lew, Chiquita, and JD, Karen and Isaac, Pennsylvania Bil, Phil and Dick, freckled Laura, sibilant Sydney, and one lustrous Pearl.

Last, in more ways than I wish were so, I want to say thank you and farewell to Gordon Sherman. He was a friend, my best. He was and always will be my mentor in business. It was Gordon who, bedridden during the last six weeks of his life, and in great discomfort, read and reread the manuscript, contributing large chunks of ideas, insight, and humor. Not only then, but during the prior years, Gordy was the pre-author, the source of so many of my thoughts and ideas that there is no proper way to acknowledge him. Although my debt to him in this book is vast, Gordy's friends know that his own book would have scintillated with a towering intellect that cannot be matched here. He had the rarest of all qualities in a businessman—courage, both personal and moral. As the head of the then NYSE-listed Midas Muffler, he gave important grants to an unknown lawyer concerned with auto safety—Ralph Nader. In Chicago, he started Businessmen Against the War to protest our presence in Vietnam, and he founded a public interest law firm. He spoke tirelessly against the duplicities of our world, without regard to the cowering hesitancy of his corporate peers. His was not an institutional courage of thinly veiled self-interest, but a personal fight for decency and commonsense. As a businessman, he will be remembered not merely for the commercial institutions he left behind, but for the heart, love, and life he inspired in those of us who were blessed to know him. Although my writing contains not a trace of his eloquence, he speaks in this book.

INDEX